BUY NOW

33 1/3 Global

33 1/3 Global, a series related to but independent from **33 1/3**, takes the format of the original series of short, music-based books and brings the focus to music throughout the world. With initial volumes focusing on Japanese and Brazilian music, the series will also include volumes on the popular music of Australia/Oceania, Europe, Africa, the Middle East, and more.

33 1/3 Japan

Series Editor: Noriko Manabe

Spanning a range of artists and genres—from the 1970s rock of Happy End to technopop band Yellow Magic Orchestra, the Shibuya-kei of Cornelius, classic anime series *Cowboy Bebop*, J-Pop/EDM hybrid Perfume, and vocaloid star Hatsune Miku—**33 1/3 Japan** is a series devoted to in-depth examination of Japanese popular music of the twentieth and twenty-first centuries.

Published Titles:

Supercell's *Supercell* by Keisuke Yamada
AKB48 by Patrick W. Galbraith and Jason G. Karlin
Yoko Kanno's *Cowboy Bebop Soundtrack* by Rose Bridges
Perfume's *Game* by Patrick St. Michel
Cornelius's *Fantasma* by Martin Roberts
Joe Hisaishi's *My Neighbor Totoro: Soundtrack* by Kunio Hara
Shonen Knife's *Happy Hour* by Brooke McCorkle
Nenes' *Koza Dabasa* by Henry Johnson
Yuming's *The 14th Moon* by Lasse Lehtonen
Toshiko Akiyoshi-Lew Tabackin Big Band's *Kogun* by E. Taylor Atkins
S.O.B.'s *Don't Be Swindle* by Mahon Murphy and Ran Zwigenberg

Forthcoming Titles:

Kohaku utagassen: The Red and White Song Contest by Shelley Brunt
Yellow Magic Orchestra's *Yellow Magic Orchestra* by Toshiyuki Ohwada

33 1/3 Brazil

Series Editor: Jason Stanyek

Covering the genres of samba, tropicália, rock, hip hop, forró, bossa nova, heavy metal and funk, among others, **33 1/3 Brazil** is a series devoted to in-depth examination of the most important Brazilian albums of the twentieth and twenty-first centuries.

Published Titles:

Caetano Veloso's *A Foreign Sound* by Barbara Browning
Tim Maia's *Tim Maia Racional Vols. 1 &2* by Allen Thayer
João Gilberto and Stan Getz's *Getz/Gilberto* by Brian McCann
Gilberto Gil's *Refazenda* by Marc A. Hertzman
Dona Ivone Lara's *Sorriso Negro* by Mila Burns
Milton Nascimento and Lô Borges's *The Corner Club* by Jonathon Grasse
Racionais MCs' *Sobrevivendo no Inferno* by Derek Pardue
Naná Vasconcelos's *Saudades* by Daniel B. Sharp
Chico Buarque's First *Chico Buarque* by Charles A. Perrone

Forthcoming Titles:

Jorge Ben Jor's *África Brasil* by Frederick J. Moehn

33 1/3 Europe

Series Editor: Fabian Holt

Spanning a range of artists and genres, **33 1/3 Europe** offers engaging accounts of popular and culturally significant albums of Continental Europe and the North Atlantic from the twentieth and twenty-first centuries.

Published Titles:

Darkthrone's *A Blaze in the Northern Sky* by Ross Hagen
Ivo Papazov's *Balkanology* by Carol Silverman
Heiner Müller and Heiner Goebbels's *Wolokolamsker Chaussee* by Philip V. Bohlman

Modeselektor's *Happy Birthday!* by Sean Nye
Mercyful Fate's *Don't Break the Oath* by Henrik Marstal
Bea Playa's *I'll Be Your Plaything* by Anna Szemere and András Rónai
Various Artists' *DJs do Guetto* by Richard Elliott
Czesław Niemen's *Niemen Enigmatic* by Ewa Mazierska and Mariusz Gradowski
Massada's *Astaganaga* by Lutgard Mutsaers
Los Rodriguez's *Sin Documentos* by Fernán del Val and Héctor Fouce
Édith Piaf's *Récital 1961* by David Looseley
Nuovo Canzoniere Italiano's *Bella Ciao* by Jacopo Tomatis
Iannis Xenakis's *Persepolis* by Aram Yardumian
Vopli Vidopliassova's *Tantsi* by Maria Sonevytsky
Amália Rodrigues's *Amália at the Olympia* by Lila Ellen Gray
Ardit Gjebrea's *Projekt Jon* by Nicholas Tochka
Aqua's *Aquarium* by C.C. McKee
J.M.K.E.'s *To the Cold Land* by Brigitta Davidjants
Taco Hemingway's *Jarmark* by Kamila Rymajdo

Forthcoming Titles:
Tripes' *Kefali Gemato Hrisafi* by Dafni Tragaki
Silly's *Februar* by Michael Rauhut
CCCP's *Fedeli Alla Linea's 1964-1985 Affinità-Divergenze Fra Il Compagno Togliatti E Noi Del Conseguimento Della Maggiore Età* by Giacomo Bottà

33 1/3 Oceania

Series Editors: Jon Stratton (senior editor) and Jon Dale (specializing in books on albums from Aotearoa/New Zealand)

Spanning a range of artists and genres from Australian Indigenous artists to Māori and Pasifika artists, from Aotearoa/New Zealand noise music to Australian rock, and including music from Papua and other Pacific islands, **33 1/3 Oceania** offers exciting accounts of albums that illustrate the wide range of music made in the Oceania region.

Published Titles:
John Farnham's *Whispering Jack* by Graeme Turner
The Church's *Starfish* by Chris Gibson
Regurgitator's *Unit* by Lachlan Goold and Lauren Istvandity
Kylie Minogue's *Kylie* by Adrian Renzo and Liz Giuffre
Alastair Riddell's *Space Waltz* by Ian Chapman
Hunters & Collectors's *Human Frailty* by Jon Stratton
The Front Lawn's *Songs from the Front Lawn* by Matthew Bannister
Bic Runga's *Drive* by Henry Johnson
The Dead C's *Clyma est mort* by Darren Jorgensen
Ed Kuepper's *Honey Steel's Gold* by John Encarnacao
Chain's *Toward the Blues* by Peter Beilharz
Hilltop Hoods' *The Calling* by Dianne Rodger
Screamfeeder's *Kitten Licks* by Ben Green and Ian Rogers
The Clean's *Boodle Boodle Boodle* by Geoff Stahl
The Avalanches' *Since I Left You* by Charles Fairchild
John Sangster's *Lord of the Rings Vols. 1–3* by Bruce Johnson
Soundtrack from *Saturday Night Fever* by Clinton Walker
Eyeliner's *BUY NOW* by Michael Brown
TISM's *Machiavelli and the Four Seasons* by Tyler Jenke

Forthcoming Titles:
The Triffids' *Born Sandy Devotional* by Christina Ballico
Crowded House's *Together Alone* by Barnaby Smith
5MMM's *Compilation Album of Adelaide Bands 1980* by Collette Snowden
INXS' *Kick* by Ryan Daniel and Lauren Moxey
Sunnyboys' *Sunnyboys* by Stephen Bruel
silverchair's *Frogstomp* by Jay Daniel Thompson
The La De Das' *The Happy Prince* by John Tebbutt
Gary Shearston's *Dingo* by Peter Mills
Kate Ceberano's *Brave* by Panizza Allmark
Robert Forster's *Danger in the Past* by Patrick Chapman

Various Artists' *A Truckload of Sky: The Lost Songs of David McComb* by Glenn D'Cruz

Dinah Lee's *Introducing Dinah Lee* by Kimberly Cannady

The Waifs' *Up All Night* by Rebecca Bennison

33 1/3 South Asia

Series Editor: Natalie Sarrazin

From the films of Bollywood and Lollywood, to home-grown *bhangra* hip-hop, Hindu devotional pop and Sufi rock, Sri Lankan rap, Indo jazz and disco, new-wave electronica and diasporic Asian Underground scene, **33 1/3 South Asia** takes readers on a sonically diverse journey through the most significant soundtracks and albums from the twentieth and twenty-first centuries.

Published:

Dil Chahta Hai Soundtrack by Jayson Beaster-Jones

Lata Mangeshkar's *My Favourites, Volume 2* by Anirudha Bhattacharjee and Chandrashekhar Rao

Coke Studio (Season 14) by Rakae Rehman Jamil and Khadija Muzaffar

Eyeliner's BUY NOW

Michael Brown

Series Editor: Jon Stratton, UniSA Creative, University of South Australia, and Jon Dale, University of Melbourne, Australia

BLOOMSBURY ACADEMIC
NEW YORK • LONDON • OXFORD • NEW DELHI • SYDNEY

BLOOMSBURY ACADEMIC
Bloomsbury Publishing Inc, 1385 Broadway,
New York, NY 10018, USA
Bloomsbury Publishing Plc, 50 Bedford
Square, London, WC1B 3DP, UK
Bloomsbury Publishing Ireland, 29 Earlsfort
Terrace, Dublin 2, D02 AY28, Ireland

BLOOMSBURY, BLOOMSBURY ACADEMIC and the Diana logo are trademarks of Bloomsbury Publishing Plc

First published in the United States of America 2025

Copyright © Michael Brown, 2025

For legal purposes the Acknowledgments on p.xii constitute an extension of this copyright page.

All rights reserved. No part of this publication may be: i) reproduced or transmitted in any form, electronic or mechanical, including photocopying, recording or by means of any information storage or retrieval system without prior permission in writing from the publishers; or ii) used or reproduced in any way for the training, development or operation of artificial intelligence (AI) technologies, including generative AI technologies. The rights holders expressly reserve this publication from the text and data mining exception as per Article 4(3) of the Digital Single Market Directive (EU) 2019/790.

Bloomsbury Publishing Inc does not have any control over, or responsibility for, any third-party websites referred to or in this book. All internet addresses given in this book were correct at the time of going to press. The author and publisher regret any inconvenience caused if addresses have changed or sites have ceased to exist, but can accept no responsibility for any such changes.

Whilst every effort has been made to locate copyright holders the publishers would be grateful to hear from any person(s) not here acknowledged.

Library of Congress Cataloging-in-Publication Data

Names: Brown, Michael, 1970- author.
Title: Buy now / Michael Brown.
Other titles: Eyeliner's Buy now
Description: [1.] | New York: Bloomsbury Academic, 2025. | Series: 33 1/3 Oceania | Includes bibliographical references and index. | Summary:
"Brimming over with fake wind-chimes, dreamy synth pads, and hyperactiveslap-bass, Eyeliner's Buy Now is an ebullient homage to the kitsch sounds of the 80s and 90s. It epitomizes a new kind of album for our times: DIY, all-digital, free, licensed as Creative Commons, and belonging to a "virtual" genre, an internet-based scene without geographic center. Drawing on the album's production archive and interviews with Rowell, this book argues that Buy Now offers both musical pleasure and mental survival-training for an era when sincerity and irony can appear dangerously indistinguishable"– Provided by publisher.
Identifiers: LCCN 2024037806 (print) | LCCN 2024037807 (ebook) | ISBN 9781501394997 (paperback) | ISBN 9781501395000 (hardback) | ISBN 9781501397837 (ebook) | ISBN 9781501397820 (pdf)
Subjects: LCSH: Eyeliner (Musician). Buy now. | Vaporwave (Music)– New Zealand–History and criticism.
Classification: LCC ML410.E97 B76 2025 (print) | LCC ML410.E97 (ebook) | DDC 781.6480993–dc23/eng/20240906
LC record available at https://lccn.loc.gov/2024037806
LC ebook record available at https://lccn.loc.gov/2024037807

ISBN: HB: 978-1-5013-9500-0
PB: 978-1-5013-9499-7
ePDF: 978-1-5013-9782-0
eBook: 978-1-5013-9783-7

Series: 33 1/3 Oceania

Typeset by Deanta Global Publishing Services, Chennai, India
Printed and bound in the United States of America

For product safety related questions contact productsafety@bloomsbury.com.

To find out more about our authors and books visit www.bloomsbury.com and sign up for our newsletters.

For Billie and Harriet

Contents

Acknowledgments xii

Introduction 1

1 **Synthesizer Pop Music since Y2K** 15

2 **Vaporwave** 33

3 **Virtual LARPing in the Musical Past** 57

4 ***BUY NOW*** 79

5 **Showbiz** 109

Conclusion 131

References 133
Index 143

Acknowledgments

This book was written in 2023 while I was JD Stout Fellow at Victoria University of Wellington. Thanks to the Stout Centre for New Zealand Studies for their invaluable support and to the Alexander Turnbull Library for their encouragement. For their kind assistance, thanks to Chris Cudby, Simon Ward, Fraser Austin, Duncan Haynes, Steven Loveridge, Dave Wilson, Geoff Stahl, Mike Lloyd, Nick Bollinger, James Gardner, Julie Fenwick, Sterling Campbell, Kate Perry, Adam Harper, and Diane McAllen. My gratitude also extends to Jon Dale and Bloomsbury. Special thanks to Luke Rowell for all his help. Unless otherwise noted, quotations are from an interview conducted with Luke in Lower Hutt, June 24 and 30, 2022.

Since its release, Eyeliner's album has sometimes been referred to as *BUY NOW*, sometimes as *Buy Now*; here I have used the first version.

Online resources to accompany this title are available at: https://www.bloomsbury.com/us/eyeliners-buy-now-9781501394997/. If you experience any problems, please contact Bloomsbury at: onlineresources@bloomsbury.com

Introduction

In February 2023, *Billboard* magazine reported that a "tidal wave" of music was hitting Internet streaming services. Every day, an estimated 100,000 tracks were being added, with new AI technology generating its own deluge, one app apparently "churning out around 17 million songs each month" for social media users.[1] Such material was on top of the tens of millions of older tracks already available. This vast ocean of instantly accessible music is just one outcome of the advent of the Internet and the wider digital revolution of the last forty years. What impact has this new environment had on contemporary music artists, especially those who came of age during the period? How have the production, distribution, consumption, and reception of music changed? Has the early utopian promise of digital technology been fulfilled?

This book tells the story of an album that bears the imprint of technological change on many levels: *BUY NOW* by Eyeliner, an alias of Aotearoa-New Zealand musician Luke Rowell. With its sumptuous tributes to advertising themes and television soundtracks, to hold music and forgotten pop genres, it's an album that rejoices in the hi-tech sounds Luke heard growing up, recreated using sophisticated twenty-first-century computer software. Released in 2015 by the US

---

[1] Leight 2023.

online label Beer on the Rug, *BUY NOW* originally came out as a digital download and mail-order cassette. It was soon acclaimed within an Internet subculture of fans and artists as an outstanding example of a new style: vaporwave. *BUY NOW* has since been reissued several times by other labels, including in a Deluxe Edition, and on various physical formats.

Nothing is quite what it seems with *BUY NOW*. Hints of the album's beguiling qualities become evident on the first encounter. For starters, the title might strike one as something of a misnomer. Sure, there are editions for sale, but anybody can have it for free online. The cover artwork's hieroglyph of a happy face is also slyly deceptive. Take a closer look at those deadpan eyes and the lopsided grin: Is that an innocent smile or a knowing smirk? Press "play" and fresh questions might arise. Out of the speakers comes an evocation of 1980s digital funk and synthesizer razzamatazz, lovingly reconstructed, but also featuring some of that era's kitschiest musical flavors: slap bass, dreamy synth pads, "doo-doo" keyboard vocal samples, and more. One might scan the track titles—"High Heels," "Sneakers for Men," "Pinot Noir," "Pictionary," "Venetian Blinds," and the rest—and wonder: Is this an album or an advertising catalog? The alias Eyeliner also fits the consumerist theme; perhaps they are the master brand on offer here. As we will see, the deeper one digs into *BUY NOW*'s background, production, and individual tracks, the more its intriguing sensibility comes into focus.

So, what is vaporwave? An experimental electronic music style that emerged in the early 2010s, it remains a quintessential example of various "Internet genres" that have appeared online over the last twenty years. Vaporwave artists take their inspiration from the consumerism, technological optimism, and corporate branding of the late 1980s and 1990s, including certain ubiquitous musical idioms of that period: shopping-mall Muzak, advertising soundtracks, classic-hits radio, smooth jazz, and new age. Some artists rework samples of these into surreal short loops, slowing down and sonically weathering them in a chopped-and-screwed style; others create gleaming all-original replicas. The vaporwave aesthetic extends to visuals too, drawing upon commercial imagery and computer graphics of similar vintage. Album titles and artist names (typically pseudonymous) round out the retro-futurist vibe, with examples including *Modern Business Collection* by INTERNET CLUB (2012), *Home*™ by PrismCorp Virtual Enterprises (2013), and *Palm Mall* by 猫 シ Corp. (2014).

The vaporwave subculture initially congregated on websites such as 4Chan, Tumblr, and Reddit. It was here in 2012 that Eyeliner was first identified as an important exponent with their album *High Fashion Mood Music* (2012), soon to be followed by *LARP of Luxury* (2013). Eyeliner's music bears many of the genre's prime traits: a fascination for lost byways of 1980s and 1990s music, deft allusions to pop culture, and an inscrutable blend of sincerity and irony. But from the start, they carved out their own niche, with a preference for all-original sample-free compositions and a pristine MIDI-based sound. If the first two albums established proof of concept for this style, *BUY NOW* was the next-generation product, Eyeliner's masterpiece.

Vaporwave has been the subject of much critical discussion. In a seminal 2012 article, UK writer Adam Harper argued that the genre was in effect a critique of contemporary capitalism, of how the consumerism of the 1980s now pervades our horizons and pre-empts all alternatives.² Such appraisals are counterbalanced though, by the evident warmth expressed by artists and fans for the dated utopias of decades past. The oft-used description of vaporwave as "music optimized for abandoned malls" captures something of this blend of nostalgia, homage, and ironic satire that is evident throughout *BUY NOW*. Even the idea of vaporwave being a genre at all carries a hint of mischief, with the name often being explained as a pun on the 1980s tech term "vaporware": software that is promoted ahead of release but never appears. The impression that vaporwave operates more like a meme is reinforced by its ever-expanding family of spinoff subcategories, including future funk, vaportrap, mallsoft, late-night lo-fi, signalwave, and utopian virtual (with which Eyeliner's music is often identified). In such ways, vaporwave knowingly plays with the viral logic of the Internet age.

The ongoing recognition that *BUY NOW* has received since its 2015 release is also notable given the "tidal wave" of creativity that vaporwave has itself experienced. In December 2016, Bandcamp, a website that enables independent artists and labels to distribute music, reported that 7,710 new albums had been given the genre tag "vaporwave" that year.[3] One vaporwave web-archive now contains over 44,000 examples. The online community itself has experienced similar growth. For instance, from a handful of early subscribers in 2012, including Luke himself, the r/vaporwave subreddit now has hundreds of thousands of members. Mainstream music has

---
[2] Harper 2012a.
[3] "2016: The Year in Stats."

also felt the genre's influence. Yet vaporwave remains largely an underground scene. As Andrew Whelan observes, the genre operates as a "distributed creative experiment," wherein thousands of anonymous artists share their productions across the social networks of the World Wide Web.[4]

To date, vaporwave has generally been written about as a placeless Internet phenomenon populated by artists hiding behind mysterious corporate pseudonyms. As the creator behind Eyeliner has never been a secret, *BUY NOW* presents the opportunity to tell a different kind of vaporwave story: that of an individual musician developing their style within the contexts of life, career, and location. Before Eyeliner, Luke had for ten years built a national profile in New Zealand as the chiptune-synthpop solo act Disasteradio. By 2012, he had already released eight Disasteradio albums, performed hundreds of gigs, and toured internationally, a background that naturally informs his subsequent vaporwave music. *BUY NOW* was itself created in a draughty loft in New Zealand's capital city, Wellington, a real-world setting that is also integral to the album's story. And while *BUY NOW* purveys a musical lingua-franca that is essentially global, it also contains submerged local references that might only be understood by New Zealanders.

The New Zealand context of *BUY NOW* also provides a useful vantage point to survey something of the Internet's impact on music. One consequence for artists from countries on the global margins, such as New Zealand, is how the Internet has enabled them to catch the world's ear more readily. In the

---

[4] Whelan 2020: 185.

half-century between 1940 and 1990, for instance, a total of 22,560 singles appeared on the American Billboard Top 100; just 6 were by New Zealand performers.[5] While state-funded initiatives played their part in subsequently boosting international exposure, the Internet has been crucial to the recent success of Lorde (nine US chart singles since 2012) and other New Zealand artists.[6] Luke's career arc traces this shift at a more indie level. While terrestrial-based Disasteradio attained a healthy New Zealand following, it is the Internet-based music of Eyeliner that has brought him international cachet.

The influence of the Internet goes deep with Luke, revealing other ways that it is shaping contemporary music. First dialing up in 1998, aged fifteen, his approach to creating and distributing music, building a career, and his musical inspirations: all evolved to a significant degree through the medium of the Internet. It's also how he ended up on the cutting edge of a new international style, vaporwave. The changing face of the Internet over the last twenty-five years, along with its affordances and stylistic qualities, forms an important thread in BUY NOW's story.

Another major theme of this book is how vaporwave reflects the experiences of recent generations. Many of vaporwave's pioneering artists are part of a demographic identified in Western countries as millennials (a.k.a. generation Y), being born between the early 1980s and mid-1990s.[7] These include Daniel Lopatin (Oneohtrix Point Never) and James

---
[5] Dowd 2013: 127–8.
[6] Shute 2023.
[7] Duffy 2021: 17–18.

Ferraro, both important precursor influences on vaporwave, as well as Patrick Driscoll (Blank Banshee), Jornt Elzinga (猫 シ Corp), Ramona Langley (Macintosh Plus), Ryan DeRobertis (SAINT PEPSI), Robin Burnett (INTERNET CLUB), and Luke Rowell, creator of *BUY NOW*. Growing up in the twin dawns of neoliberalism and the digital age, they were all exposed in their formative years to the popular culture underlying the vaporwave aesthetic. Deep memories of this era, we will see, resonate throughout *BUY NOW*.

The musical sources that lend vaporwave its distinctive flavor are an obvious generational connection. The aural wallpaper of chain retail, television, and video games, often using synthesizers and drum machines, and blurring into popular genres of the day, formed a background soundtrack to 1980s and 1990s childhoods around the world. Such material, Adam Trainer argues, "represents the paradox of much corporatized popular culture: luridly sentimental, creatively hollow and vapid, yet aesthetically alluring."[8] Much of vaporwave's charm comes from the way it spins musical gold out of such kitsch.

Equally notable, though, is vaporwave's ambivalence toward these sources, its apparent dual affection for and lack of illusions about consumer capitalism's tacky soundtrack. "Vaporwave is never simply a celebration of kitsch," Ross Cole observes, "it's an odd kind of hip avant-garde imbued with an ironic and cutting self-awareness."[9] Studies of vaporwave have interpreted this ambivalence in a variety of ways. Adam Harper

---
[8]Trainer 2016: 413.
[9]Cole 2020: 317.

regards it as an expression of "accelerationist" politics, for instance; Padraic Killeen of "a genre of the impasse," and Laura Glitsos as "memory play."[10] This book considers vaporwave with reference to a concept used by Trainer and Cole: "postirony."[11]

Popular music's capacity for conveying irony (saying one thing and meaning the opposite) is well-known, as found in the work of Bob Dylan, Randy Newman, and Steely Dan. But what is "postirony"? It's a term that has been previously applied to bands such as Ween and the Darkness, who create "a highly subtle fusion of accepted elements of [their genres] combined with an ironic take on these."[12] In the case of vaporwave, not only individual artists, but the entire genre seems imbued with postironic attitude, even its very name. The genre has the "quantum power," Cole argues, "to exist as ... nostalgia and ironic mischief, simultaneously."[13]

Postirony—as the "post" suggests—occupies its own position in the cultural history timeline. Popular culture of the 1980s and 1990s was often characterized as suffering from an "irony epidemic."[14] TV shows such as *Seinfeld* and *The Simpsons*, the novels of Bret Easton Ellis and Tama Janowitz, and the music of Nirvana and Pavement, all were imbued with an irony that assumed a fatalistic or cynical worldview. A subsequent wave of creative artists sought to move past these jaundiced positions, to be *post*ironic. As Lee Konstantinou discusses, certain novelists (such as David Foster Wallace and Dave

---

[10] Harper 2012a; Killeen 2018; Glitsos 2018.
[11] Trainer 2016; Cole 2020.
[12] Bennett 2013: 210.
[13] Cole 2020: 311.
[14] Young 1994: 6.

Eggers) and filmmakers (such as Wes Anderson and Charlie Kaufman) found ways to escape the impasse of an irony-saturated culture.[15] Without reverting to simple earnestness, they temper irony with sincerity, quirkiness, or a sense of enchantment.

Vaporwave can be regarded as its own species of postironic art, responding to similar cultural challenges but from a later generation's perspective. Luke's music is a good illustration. While influenced by sarcastic culture-jammers like Devo and Negativland that he was exposed to as a teenager, it equally embraces the optimism and allure of the popular culture he grew up with. Eyeliner achieves an especially subtle fusion of irony and sincerity. "It's like I'm trying to be like perfectly between," he told me in 2022.

Also cropping up in *BUY NOW*'s backstory are social phenomena that Konstantinou sees as encouraging postironic sensibilities. These include the gig economy that has flourished under neoliberalism, supplanting what were previously permanent jobs, including in the creative sector.[16] Under previous employment regimes, workers could adopt an ironic outlook to put some distance between work roles and their "authentic beliefs." Now, Konstantinou suggests that as contractors and fixed-term employees move between projects, they must cultivate "sincere commitment, intrinsic motivation and earnest engagement" for each job at hand while it lasts, and then "exhibit the flexibility, openness to contingency and

---
[15] Konstantinou 2016.
[16] See Klein 2001: 255–84.

self-ironising capacities to move on to the next endeavour."[17] For workers caught in this quicksand of "contingent belief," a postironic attitude, a mindset that allows them to nimbly navigate between sincerity and irony, has much practical use. Our relationship with consumer goods can be similarly complicated. Branded clothing and footwear—to take some obvious examples—have come to be marketed and acquired as expressions of each consumer's personal identity. As Steven Shaviro notes, while some might be inclined to regard this idea ironically, they are still required to make such choices (the only alternative being to fabricate one's own apparel). "Our ironic detachment," he observes, "is the very thing that allows us to continue doing the things we are being ironic about."[18]

Vaporwave is music that makes a kind of hip pleasure out of such ambiguities. Like other postironic art, it reveals "a desire . . . for the unco-optable, an ethos or sensibility that, in its constitution, can never lose its oppositional flavour . . . an art object that never loses its cool."[19] Vaporwave can be regarded as a major contribution to popular music by a generation peculiarly sensitized to the paradoxes of contemporary life.

The millennials and their successors, gen-Z, are also far more globalized than earlier generations. "[New] communications technologies," Bobby Duffy points out, "provide many more ways to share experiences across national boundaries."[20] The global vaporwave subculture is a salient example of the new kinds of communities brought about by the Internet. Two

---

[17] Konstantinou 2017: 102.
[18] Shaviro 2006: 10.
[19] Konstantinou 2016: 229.
[20] Duffy 2021: 22.

other aspects of the digital revolution integral to the story of *BUY NOW* can also be highlighted.

First, there is technology's impact on how music is created. Making recordings with high production values once required expensive studios and equipment. The situation began to change in the 1980s with the arrival of affordable synthesizers, samplers, and sequencers. Early on, Andrew Goodwin identified these as leading to an increased "democratization" of music production.[21] Personal computers accelerated the trend, with sophisticated software now readily accessible to anybody with a laptop. Such democracy of means is intrinsic to the aesthetics and ethics of Luke's music. Consequently, this book delves extensively into the technology used to create *BUY NOW*. It also considers a flipside, how the "timbral conformity" (Goodwin's term) of 1980s synthesizers gave rise to the perceived kitschiness that Eyeliner's music also feeds off.

When dealing with an album called *BUY NOW*, the economics of digital music is another obvious topic. Music is often presented as the classic demonstration of the Internet's disruptive power. Beginning in 1999 with the launch of Napster, this narrative is generally depicted as a running battle between the traditional recording industry and file-sharing pirates.[22] Luke's career and *BUY NOW* fit into an adjacent history of small labels, independent distribution websites, physical releases, and the open-licensing system of Creative Commons. It's a world of free enterprise opportunity, but also precarity. The plight of the indie artist in the digital age is one reason

---
[21] Goodwin 1992.
[22] Allen-Robertson 2013.

why Luke finds the capitalism-critical streak in vaporwave a necessary reality check, even if some other artists have downplayed this early interpretation of the genre.

Lastly, some words about my involvement with Luke's music and the "bonus track" that goes with this book. Starting in 2018, I got to know Luke in my capacity as Music Curator at the Alexander Turnbull Library (part of the National Library of New Zealand). Over the next few years, we collaborated on a project to address the challenge of preserving digital music productions given the ongoing obsolescence of software, operating systems, and computer hardware. *BUY NOW* was our first test case.[23]

The archival problems were not my only interest, though. As a gen-Xer, twelve years older than Luke, I was intrigued by vaporwave. Here were mainstream sounds from my teenage and early adult years being reinterpreted by a generation for whom they obviously didn't carry quite the same baggage. (Back then, I'd soon headed for indie rock, and looked back to 1960s and 1970s music.) Vaporwave also led me to think about the history of the Internet, which had arrived at different stages in our lives, with very different consequences. Internet history will inevitably roll onward and much of what is discussed here will become out of date. But as a book about an early digital native's music, written from the perspective of somebody who reached adulthood in the pre-Internet world, it represents a certain moment that won't come again.

The outcome of the Turnbull Library project was an archive containing MIDI arrangements, stems (separate audio for

---

[23] Brown 2021.

instrumental parts), mixes, and other documentation, for every track on *BUY NOW*. This book has benefited greatly from access to this material. The archive is also available for you—the reader—to access at any time through the library's website.[24] What's more, it can all be downloaded under a Creative Commons license, so you can create your own remixes or explore the innermost circuitry of the album that is the subject of this book.

---

[24] Material from "Buy Now" (ref. Series-6711), Alexander Turnbull Library: https://tiaki.natlib.govt.nz/#details=ecatalogue.1033472.

1 Synthesizer Pop Music since Y2K

Luke Rowell's oldest memory is musical. It was a rainy night when his father took him down to a nearby shopping mall to pick up a new Sherwood hi-fi system. Back home, they set it up in the lounge. As Luke recalls:

> The first record I remember him ever putting on and the first time I remember recorded music being played, he picked me up over a copy of *Switched-On Bach*, the [1968] Wendy Carlos record. At the time I would have been five or six years old. There was this kind of moment. I remember seeing the blue label of CBS Records turning around and this synthesizer music coming out.

It's a primal recollection that presages a future devoted to the sounds of synthesizers.

Luke was born in 1983 in the city of Lower Hutt (pop. 95,000), across Wellington Harbour from New Zealand's capital, Wellington. The family lived in what he recalls as "a little draughty roughcast Deco house" in Lower Hutt's leafy central suburbia, a few blocks from the downtown shops. He was the youngest of three siblings to two working parents. His father was a civil engineer turned glazier, and his mother was a teacher of children convalescing at the nearby hospital.

To fully understand Luke's vaporwave roots, we need to start with some personal background. This chapter explores his early musical enthusiasms and encounters with computers. Along the way, it examines the Lower Hutt context and the socioeconomic changes of the 1980s and 1990s, including the Internet's arrival. The chapter concludes with the Disasteradio years, just before vaporwave was booted into existence.

"Rowell grew up in a family with interests that met at the intersection of art and technology," Martyn Pepperell observes.[1] His mother did interpretative dance; both older siblings had musical inclinations, taking lessons. Luke's father came from a family that included both scientists—an uncle became an MIT professor—and musicians. His paternal grandfather (who died before Luke was born) had run a dancehall in Wellington where he'd played drums, going on to manage the scenic workshop at one of New Zealand's first television stations and becoming a skilled animator.

Family life also included a vein of humor that crops up throughout Luke's music. "My parents were doing community theatre and I'd go see my dad, you know, singing in a tutu . . . camp pantomime stuff." Another family LP that fascinated him was *More Hot Butter* (1973), by US synthesizer group Hot Butter (of "Popcorn" fame). Likewise created with a Moog, the album complemented the classical strains of *Switched-On Bach*. It represented synthesizer music's potential for liberating fun.

Computers arrived early. When Luke was six, a Commodore 64 (C64) turned up at the family home. He was enthralled. The most popular home computer of all time, the C64 was readily

---

[1] Pepperell 2021.

programmable and had numerous games available. Games became a major focus of his circle of friends, who took turns hosting sessions on the different systems each had at home.

The pulsing arpeggios and looping melodies of game soundtracks got into his brain. The C64 featured the innovative SID sound chip developed by the team who later founded the synthesizer company Ensoniq. "That was definitely very formative on my practice as a computer musician," Luke remembers. He began to put on game soundtracks for background listening: "If I had to clean my room as a kid, I'd load up . . . just leave them running." Later, when he got a Walkman, he recorded mixtapes off the C64 speaker using a boombox so his soundtrack of choice could accompany him everywhere.[2]

Formal schooling could hardly compete. "I was always waiting to go home to then work on my little projects, my computer programming or musical electronics things," Luke remembers. "For whatever reason I wouldn't trust a lot of teachers as authority figures, often [getting] into trouble." A born autodidact, his ambivalent relationship with education would continue into later years.

Luke considers television to be the other main cultural influence of his childhood, particularly American shows: "I deeply love American culture." The diet of after-school shows included *Teenage Mutant Ninja Turtles* and *Gargoyles*, while evening sessions with his siblings encompassed series such as *Quantum Leap*, *MacGyver*, and *Star Trek: Next Generation*. Darker-themed viewing—*The X-Files*, *Twin Peaks*, *Unsolved*

---
[2]Smithies 2011.

Mysteries, video dubs of *Predator* and *RoboCop*—left an impression too. "I was allowed to watch as much TV as I liked," Luke says, "[b]ecause I was the youngest and everything was sort of happening around me." He was not alone. New Zealand children were heavy consumers of television in this era. Nine-year-olds watched an average 2.6 hours a day according to a 1991 international survey, second only to American children.[3]

As well as soaking up the scenarios and visuals, Luke got hooked on television's musical soundtrack of theme tunes, incidental scores, and advertising jingles ("a whole bunch of ads got stuck in my head"). His sonic curiosity also took in the wider environment. Dings in elevators, vehicle reversing beepers, sirens: Where did they come from and how were they made?

Inner suburban and downtown Lower Hutt, with its shops, malls, and arcades, formed Luke's home turf during adolescence. It was a strikingly modern environment, much of the city having been built since a burst of utopian socialist planning in the 1930s and 1940s.

Given vaporwave's utopian themes and the historical subtext of Luke's first experiment with the style (see Chapter 2), it is worth noting that Lower Hutt has several times served as a blank canvas for such social dreaming. It was here in 1840 that the New Zealand Company began the British colonization of New Zealand, eulogizing the Hutt Valley in advertisements back in London as a "LAND of PROMISE" and site of "future Villas

---

[3] Purves and Elley 1994: 101.

and Country Mansions."[4] Natural disasters intervened, however, and there were also fears of conflict between colonial forces and Māori, the indigenous inhabitants of Aotearoa-New Zealand. Use of the valley was subsequently limited largely to farming and pleasure gardens for picnicking Wellingtonians. The canvas essentially remained blank.

Then, in 1936, the First Labour Government embarked on the largest state housing project in New Zealand history: Lower Hutt would become the country's foremost example of a planned city. Within a few decades, the valley was blanketed with houses. By 1975, Lower Hutt was, for its size, an industrial, scientific, and cultural powerhouse. Along with a booming manufacturing sector, it had become a location for Department of Scientific Industrial Research (DSIR) centers and the New Zealand Broadcasting Corporation's studio tower complex in the suburb of Avalon. Luke's grandfather had worked at Avalon Studios, living nearby. "Up in my grandma's . . . looking at those diamond lights," Luke recalls. "We called them 'the UFOs.' It's like this Dalek in the middle of Avalon."

By the early 1990s, Luke was venturing out with friends, increasingly drawn to the buzz of downtown Lower Hutt. It was, in his words, "popping off." There were video arcades, cinemas, and a trading card shop. "You could spend a Thursday night on late-night shopping and just be there for hours," he remembers. "Go hang out at the comic shop . . . [which would be] filled with a whole bunch of guys that my brother knew . . . older dudes." These excursions invariably finished up at

---

[4] Burns 1989: 109.

Queensgate, the first and largest mega-mall in the Wellington region, opened in 1986 and expanded several times since.

> Growing up in the Hutt, the whole epicenter of Queensgate, I remember that. No matter where you would set out for, you would end up in Queensgate. To the point where one of my little insomnia rituals is to recreate Queensgate in my mind in different eras, knowing which shops were where . . . There was something very idealistic and convenient about everything in Queensgate.

Shopping malls, personal computers, video games, US television, and home video: all these helped define childhood for Luke and his generation more broadly. They also signified profound changes sweeping through New Zealand and across the world, transformations that were partly technological, the first steps of the digital revolution to come, but also economic.

New Zealand's highly protected and state-controlled economy had begun to falter in the mid-1970s. Inflation, national debt, and unemployment all rose. In 1984, as a monetary crisis loomed, the newly elected Fourth Labour Government steered the country toward *laissez-faire* neoliberal solutions. Its policies—and those of subsequent governments—brought New Zealand into sync with an emerging global economy defined by the idea that free trade and free markets were the most efficient mechanisms for the allocation of goods and services. Financial markets were deregulated, import tariffs slashed, state agencies were restructured as commercial enterprises or sold off, and taxes were cut. While similar agendas were implemented elsewhere, notably in Ronald Reagan's America and Margaret Thatcher's

Britain, New Zealand took one of the most comprehensive approaches: in 1988, *The Economist* magazine dubbed the country "Adam Smith's islands," after the eighteenth-century founder of modern capitalism.[5]

There were obvious downsides for small cities such as Lower Hutt. Traditional manufacturing slumped and unemployment, fueled by the effects of the 1987 stock market crash, continued to rise. The DSIR centers downsized and the use of Avalon Studios withered away as operations transferred elsewhere or were outsourced to private companies.

But New Zealand was also waking up to opportunities it had missed during the protectionist era. The availability of consumer products and luxury goods increased dramatically. New media outlets and service industries emerged. By the mid-1990s, New Zealand's rate of adopting modern technology had surged to equal that of the United States, even exceeding it in the case of personal computers and Internet connections.[6]

Consumption patterns also shifted toward American-style consumerism. Trading hours were extended and huge new shopping centers were built. Such centers not only sold goods but also sold "consumption" itself. The very act of shopping became an entertainment experience, proving a huge drawcard. A 1991 survey of New Zealanders' recreational activity found that shopping malls had become the most popular leisure destination, even ahead of beaches and restaurants.[7] The purpose of consumer choices also changed,

---

[5]"Adam Smith's Islands."
[6]Galt 2022: 91–2.
[7]Hillary Commission 1991: 17.

with brands becoming part of "the processes by which our identities are shaped."[8] A joke from the period, "I shop therefore I am," was only half-ironic.

The Queensgate mega-mall was Lower Hutt's most obvious success story coming out of this revolution. Where Wellingtonians seeking recreation in the 1880s had flocked to the Hutt's pleasure gardens, a century later they hit the mall. And, in its way, Queensgate represented the Hutt Valley's latest utopia: a paradise of consumption that offered vestiges of collectivism—a public plaza filled with amenities—originally envisaged of all shopping malls by their inventor, Austrian architect and socialist Victor Gruen.[9]

Yet Queensgate itself cast long shadows. The mega-mall blighted traditional retail in surrounding streets, which are to this day dotted with empty shopfronts. Nearby too is Lower Hutt's own abandoned mall, Centre City Plaza, a smaller competitor slowly crushed by Queensgate's economies of scale.

Luke's interest in popular music began at age eleven. He remembers his older brother Tom one day catching his attention: "Hey, listen to this band, Nirvana." Five years older than Luke, Tom hung out with a group of hardcore punk enthusiasts at Hutt Valley High School. Some would go on to form bands—such as Diecast, in which Tom sang vocals—that found an audience in the Wellington punk-revival scene.

Tom became an important source of new information. "I got a hyper-accelerated music education through him," Luke

---

[8] Kearns, Murphy, and Friesen 2001: 194.
[9] Hardwick 2004: 72–90.

later told Martyn Pepperell.[10] His brother facilitated access to wider networks too, as Luke discovered upon entering high school the year after Tom graduated: "I sort of inherited his friend group . . . a strong cassette-swapping community." It was now popular music being loaded into Luke's Walkman. Through these circles, he tapped into heavier sounds of the day: Sepultura, Butthole Surfers, Pailhead, and Mr. Bungle. He was also looking back to other periods and genres:

> There was a point where nobody was listening to synthpop . . . You would hear it on classic hits radio maybe. It was positively not liked. I remember my brother's friend . . . I was listening to Devo, and he storms into my room: "What is this? A fucking roller-disco?" . . . But as those guys went off to tertiary or wherever they were going after high school, I definitely latched onto more mid-80s synthpop.

Also steering Luke toward new musical territories was Tom's girlfriend, the artist Kerry Ann Lee. A key figure in the Wellington DIY music and arts scene, she had first introduced Luke to the New Wave band Devo. Her tip-offs also included other American culture-jammers such as Negativland and the Moog Cookbook, who covered grunge anthems in the style of the old Moog synth LPs. Another recommendation was RE/Search Publications' *Incredibly Strange Music* books about exotica, easy listening, and other overlooked genres: "She saw that I was into camp, even veering on bad taste, music."

---

[10] Pepperell 2021.

Other lines of interest were also converging. Guitar lessons ("open chord strum stuff") had begun for Luke while at primary school; he'd also spent time dabbling on his older sister Liz's Kawai FS610 home keyboard. Then, in 1995, he started with a new guitar teacher, Greg Jackson, who had a four-track recorder, computer, and General MIDI module. Jackson gave Luke a collection of music shareware on floppy disks, inducting him into the world of MOD trackers: sample-based sequencers originally invented to create Commodore Amiga game soundtracks.[11] A new door was cracking open: "My guitar teacher gives me the software that basically means that I put my guitar down and start using the computer."

Luke describes his early efforts at computer music as "noodling around." Running the MS-DOS program Digitrakker on a 386SX-25 PC, he looped samples extracted from game resource files, using the QWERTY keyboard to input notes. But with no microphone or sound card for creating new samples, the setup was limited. Yes, Luke had other gear (guitars, tape recorders), a mind alive with musical discoveries, and an older brother as a role model and entry into the Wellington scene. What he lacked was the right catalyst to kickstart his musical creativity. The Internet would soon provide it.

Information about music could be hard to come by before the Internet. Now, we can turn to Google or Wikipedia for answers, search for tracks on Spotify, or seek the wisdom of crowds in online forums. But pre-Internet, word of mouth, magazines,

---

[11] Collins 2008: 57–9.

radio, and television only got you so far in places such as Lower Hutt.

In 1989, New Zealand deregulated its telecommunications sector. Shortly afterward it became the first country in the Asia-Pacific region to be fully connected with the US Internet backbone.[12] By the mid-1990s, with the invention of user-friendly browsers such as Netscape Navigator, the World Wide Web became a truly practical proposition, and Internet usage and the creation of new websites took off.

The advent of the Internet is another defining event for Luke's generation, securing their place as the first so-called digital natives.[13] One thing the Internet offered was a new relationship to information. With instant access to knowledge on a massive scale, millennials arrived during their formative years at what philosopher Michel Serres posits as "the end of the era of experts."[14] The expanded scope for social contact was also ground-breaking. The Internet enabled real-time interaction with communities spanning the globe and all topics of interest.

Using his father's business dialup, Luke first logged onto the Internet in 1998. Google Search had just launched, and the most popular websites were the likes of AOL, Yahoo, and GeoCities. Downloading pirated games was the initial priority, but Luke was soon drawn into the world of a shareware music application called Jeskola Buzz.

---

[12] Newman 2008: 103.
[13] Prensky 2001.
[14] Serres 2015: 31.

A more sophisticated version of the trackers he'd previously used, Buzz also came with its own online community. Buzz users were based worldwide but many hailed from the European demoscene, including the application's Finnish creator, Oskari Tammelin. The demoscene was a computer subculture originating in the mid-1980s dedicated to creating "demos," audiovisual demonstrations of programming skills often appended onto "cracked" games as introductory brags,[15] which typically incorporated MOD tracker music. After downloading Jeskola Buzz to his new Pentium 166 PC (running Windows 95), Luke immersed himself in the #buzz IRC (Internet Relay Chat) channel. It was the breakthrough he needed:

> Once I was there, I was on that channel for three or four hours a day. Talking to people from Europe about all kinds of things, but also getting music recommendations. There were all these people into IDM [intelligent dance music] . . . Autechre, Boards of Canada, and Squarepusher . . . a lot of guys who are making trance . . . teaching me things about synthesis that I didn't know I needed to know . . . People talking 24/7 about it. It was cool . . . that was the big thing that made me want to make my own records.

Jeskola Buzz would serve as Luke's main creative engine for the next decade. "Through Buzz I found the best avenue for expressing the music I wanted to create," he later told Ian

---

[15]Whelan 2017: 444.

Jorgenson.[16] With a ready supply of samples, tracker files, and IRC expertise, he started composing music in earnest.

The Internet was also where Luke released the first results. In his final term at high school, he began uploading tracks to the MP3.com website. It was 2000, the year commemorated in Luke's long-standing Bandcamp by-line "Synthesizer pop music since Y2K."

MP3.com was the first of many music-distribution platforms Luke would employ in the era before iTunes and Spotify. They all tended to be sites that enabled free downloads. He would continue to encourage the free sharing of his music, later adopting the Creative Commons open-licensing system (see Chapter 5). He later credited this stance to the Wellington punk and DIY music scene,[17] but he'd also been inspired by technological utopianism:

> I saw a mindset of technology in the early 90s, with things like MIT's Media Lab . . . [the TV series] *Beyond 2000*, and the early Internet and bulletin board systems, where it's a very open access, free for all . . . everybody's giving what they can, and everybody takes what they want. I've always thought that the future would be like that.

Hanging out on the IRC channel, he'd gone on to collaborate on designing and testing open-source enhancements for Jeskola Buzz, and he wanted to be similarly open in sharing his music with the world.

---

[16] Blink 2004: 28.
[17] "Case Study: Luke Rowell."

"Disasteradio" became his chosen musical alias. The name, taken from a 1950s Japanese crystal set packaged in a mushroom cloud-emblazoned box that he had spotted in a library book, captured the "camp science" aesthetic he wanted to develop. Luke was also seeking to distinguish himself from the macho vibe of his brother's hardcore punk-revival scene. Musically, he instead looked to subversives such as Devo and contemporary electronic music groups like Add N to (X). "I wanted to have my own little pocket that I was in and that wasn't anyone else's," he remarks. The earliest Disasteradio tracks were instrumentals that drew from sounds Luke had long been enamored with: the effects and chiptune melodies of computer games, MOD-style beats, sci-fi soundtracks, and hokey vocal samples.

In 2001, Luke enrolled in computer science at Victoria University of Wellington (VUW). But ambivalence about formal education dogged him, and he soon dropped out to focus on music, surviving financially on glazing work for his father. Others were getting interested in the sounds he was creating though. Early in 2002, Kerry Ann Lee invited Luke to support US solo punkster Adam Goren (Atom and His Package) at a Wellington gig. Through her DIY mail-order service, Red Letter Distro, Lee also began selling the albums he was now producing with a CD–R burner.

Luke's musical palette was expanding, too. In 2003, he returned to Victoria University, this time to study music. The VUW School of Music had a history of technological innovation, being home to the country's oldest electronic music studio, established in 1966 by composer Douglas Lilburn. The equipment included vintage synthesizers such as a Roland System 100M and Fairlight CMI Series III, and several subsequent Disasteradio tracks were based on live 100M recordings. Further feeding his creativity was secondhand gear he began to pick up cheaply. He assembled a live-performance rig including a Commodore SX-64, backing tracks on CD–R, sound-producing toys, and old synths such as a Korg M-500 SP.

While the Internet had launched Disasteradio, Luke eventually broke through as a live act. Gigging regularly around Wellington, he secured an influential supporter in Ian Jorgensen (a.k.a. Blink). When he first caught Luke's solo act in 2003, Jorgensen was on the brink of launching A Low Hum (ALH), a magazine, record label, and promotion company that would become a major force in New Zealand indie music during the 2004–16 period.[18] "I can't even describe how much Luke stood out from the music scene at the time because nothing else has been so different since," Jorgenson later told Martyn Pepperell.[19]

Over the next ten years, ALH would book Disasteradio alongside other artists for national tours and festivals, as well as organizing dedicated tours. Recognized for his enthusiasm and ability to warm up crowds, Luke served as support for popular local bands such as the Mint Chicks and Supergroove, and, in Australia, Regurgitator. The association with Jorgenson continued with shoestring jaunts to Europe, Australia, and the United States. Between 2004 and 2012, Luke performed close to 350 gigs as Disasteradio.[20]

---

[18] Shute 2014.
[19] Pepperell 2021.
[20] Listing of gigs (2002-2021), Luke Rowell Collection.

The Disasteradio sound evolved along the way. The initial run of five albums (2002–6) explored chiptune and early synth sounds, but in the live arena, Luke was developing a more song-oriented beat-driven style. Influences here included ALH contemporaries such as Cortina, the Fanatics, and Golden Axe (featuring future vaporwave artist, Chris Cudby). Audience response was another factor. "The best times on stage were when the beat was driving properly," Luke recalls.

The results can be heard on the Disasteradio albums *Visions* (2007) and *Charisma* (2010). With their synth backings, pop hooks, and vocoder vocals, both received critical raves, *Visions* being lauded as "New Zealand Release of the Year" by magazine *Real Groove*.[21] These albums also spawned several hit videos and in 2011 Disasteradio had an online viral moment when the YouTube video for "Gravy Rainbow" (from *Charisma*) was mentioned on American comedian Daniel Tosh's *Tosh.0* blog. The attention drove up views, which soon reached 500,000 and now stand at over one million.

The mature Disasteradio style was an important precursor to the vaporwave sounds of Eyeliner that emerged the following year. Before moving on, it's worth registering some of the continuities. First, the focus is on the sounds of the 1980s. The synthpop revival was well underway by the mid-2000s, spurred on by the electroclash movement and acts such as Daft Punk.[22] But Luke brought his own idiosyncratic connoisseurship to Disasteradio. Originating in his teenage years, a love for musical deep-dives had been fed by friends

---

[21] Pepperell 2021.
[22] Reynolds 2011: 173–6.

and turbo-charged by the Internet. Italo-disco, Japanese pop groups, European synth-meisters, and new age are some of the more unusual sources that feed into both Disasteradio and Eyeliner.

The retrospective tendency that informs Eyeliner (and vaporwave more broadly) also has roots in Disasteradio. This was not simply nostalgia. Luke saw how synthpop artists such as Kraftwerk and Thomas Dolby had themselves referenced earlier historical epochs in their music, producing a timeless quality. "It feels like there is a renaissance aspect," he observes. "It looks back at something and re-subsumes it." He had attempted something similar by looking back to 80s synthpop, with Disasteradio songs juxtaposing past and future in ways which are (in his words) "contemptuous with time." Eyeliner pushes the envelope even further, producing music that—at its best—seems to stop the clock, capturing an eternal present.

A fascination with modern technology and how it shapes human experience carries over, too. This theme was personal. Luke had reckoned with his emotional attachment to computers from an early age. "I spent a bit of time in my youth being afraid of school, afraid of the world," he recalls. "Just being in my bedroom with a computer was incredibly comforting." However, he had come to appreciate that music technologies such as synthesizers are not neutral and that all sorts of assumptions are built into them about what music is meant to be. This realization plays out in baroquely complex terms on *Charisma*, but with Eyeliner, Luke went in the other direction, exploring the possibilities of just a handful of iconic instruments.

Lastly, threading through Disasteradio's music is a vein of social commentary that also informs Eyeliner. Luke was first alerted to music's potentially critical function by Devo, perhaps his single most important influence. With their roots in the 1960s counterculture, Devo had championed "the role of art in countering elements of socialization."[23] As Cristina Bodinger-deUriarte writes, Devo's work employs "irony, parody and caricature" to target the pathologies they saw in American society. "The use of an exaggerated form of the targeted assumption, carried out to its 'logical' extreme," she explains, "enables easy ridicule of the extreme presented, and then by a process of logical transference, a questioning of the original assumption."[24] A similar strategy is evident with Disasteradio songs such as "Gravy Rainbow," an upbeat anthem that is itself a satire of upbeat anthems (specifically in TV advertising). As we will see, Eyeliner shares such critical goals but reflects even more deeply on advertising music's powers of persuasion.

This chapter has laid out the backstory of Luke's pre-Eyeliner life and music, setting the scene for the rest of the book. Yet, in 2011, one might never have guessed what was coming. Disasteradio was going strong: a new album out the previous year, a viral YouTube hit, and a successful overseas tour. Luke played eighty-four shows in 2011 across Europe, North America, Australia, and New Zealand. Very soon though, his journey would veer off to parts unknown.

---

[23] Bodinger-deUriarte 1985: 57.
[24] Bodinger-deUriarte 1985: 64.

2 Vaporwave

Imagine the hot, crowded darkness of a dance club, pounding beats and warped vocals, and then stepping out a door into a well-lit, air-conditioned boutique, shoppers strolling past to the gentle strains of digital piano. To follow the final track of Disasteradio's *Charisma* (2010) with the opener of Luke's next album, Eyeliner's *High Fashion Mood Music* (2012), is to undergo just such a startling transition. We seem to have been transported to an entirely different musical sphere.

This chapter looks at Luke's artistic leap into this new style, vaporwave, and the evolution of the Eyeliner sound through to *BUY NOW*. The Internet's role in vaporwave's emergence is part of this story too, including how *High Fashion Mood Music* was quickly recognized online as an early classic. A discussion of Eyeliner's approach to vaporwave concludes the chapter. We begin in Wellington, back before vaporwave burst into life, as Luke starts to encounter the first ripples of this new style.

Since 2008, Luke had been living in a rented loft space nicknamed Skyranch, located above an inner-city panel beater. Flatmates included filmmaker Simon Ward and special-effects artist Don Brooker, both of whom were among the thousands of contractors working in Wellington for Peter Jackson's movie/digital-effects company, Weta, of *Lord of the Rings* fame. Skyranch was a hive of more low-budget activity. "We had a little collective together," Luke recalls. "A green-screen set up permanently ... bands sleeping on the couches ... filming NZ On Air-funded videos." It was here that the videos for Disasteradio's *Charisma* were shot. Creative work and freelance contracts kept everybody busy.

Five years older than Luke, Simon Ward also became a key conduit for hearing the new music that was constantly scrolling up over the Internet horizon:

> He would play a lot of music in the background while we were working together, long, ten-twelve hour days. I would do some of the grunt work ... keying and taking out tracking dots and rotoscoping stuff ... Sometime in 2011, he was playing the Computer Dreams/Napolian split on [US label] Beer on the Rug. This was before it was called "vaporwave" ... I was like: "This is incredible." ... It felt like I was hearing something that was destined to come out.

This feeling of predestination related to the Internet's evolution since the heyday of MP3.com a decade earlier. Much had changed, with the new era of Web 2.0 well underway. Blogging, social media, and the ability for users to like, share, and comment had spawned a decentralized indie-music ecology—an online underground. It was a place where dusty corners of the musical past were explored and the latest sounds quickly spread. *Altered Zones*, a 2010–11 spinoff of web magazine *Pitchfork* that aggregated blog posts from other sites, was emblematic. "There was ... music distribution and criticism, review ... the Net Art scene on Tumblr ... early computer graphics, VHS rips, GIFs," Luke recalls. The Web 2.0 environment was also a seedbed for "Internet genres," cultural styles that exist primarily online,[1] early examples having included witch house and seapunk.

Also part of vaporwave's history is a line of retro-oriented music genres that had been developing since the mid-2000s, including hauntology, hypnagogic pop, and chillwave. Georgina Born and Christopher Haworth refer to these as all being on the "nostalgia genre continuum," due to the artists' shared interest in "the recovery, re-imagination and remediation of past popular-cultural and media epochs."[2] Luke was aware of all these movements and sensed something new brewing around the time of *Altered Zones*: "We'd just been through chillwave at that point, but chillwave had this more naïve, blissful sense to it." The music of Computer Dreams seemed to herald a new phase.

What caught Luke's ear was partly an atmosphere: "hypnotic, slow, repetitive, languid, frozen-in-time music." A certain conceptual savvy clicked, too. Computer Dreams (the alias of an anonymous artist from Houston, Texas) seemed to have a heightened awareness of the history of digital media. The track "Rain," for example, which samples Dan Siegel's smooth jazz instrumental "Where Are You Now" (1984), had a low-bitrate quality, much like an MP3 from back in the 1990s when bandwidth was low and file compression high. That such digital textures could be used to historically watermark music intrigued Luke: "it has a kind of digitality to it that it's not apologizing for," he observes. "It's being it." Another release that set him thinking was US musician James Ferraro's *Far*

---
[1] Glitsos 2018: 103.
[2] Born and Haworth 2018: 625.

Side Virtual (2011), an album that used preset sounds from the macOS application GarageBand to create a shiny, cheap-sounding digital surface. Luke was fascinated, listening to the album on an almost daily basis.

Informing his perspective at this time, too, was a return to Victoria University in 2009–10. While as inconclusive as previous stints, cultural theory lectures by visiting US musicologist Chris Tonelli were a major inspiration. "If I hadn't studied musicology," Luke told an interviewer in 2014, "I don't think I would have been as interested in vaporwave."[3] The idea of *détournement* particularly caught his attention. *Détournement* (literally meaning "diversion") had been developed within the French Letterist and Situationist movements by Marxist theorist Guy Debord, the practice later influencing punk music and culture-jammers such as Negativland.[4] With a *détournement*, an existing cultural artifact is removed from its context or closely imitated for a new work, and the audience is "diverted" away from the original meaning toward perceiving a new one. Such acts often subvert the ideology of the original, as with the alteration of advertising billboards ("adbusting") by anti-corporate activists in the 1990s. The concept gave Luke new ways of thinking about certain long-standing musical inspirations and made his 2011 encounters with early vaporwave—with its samples and other *détournements*—all the more thought-provoking. He would not be alone in making these connections.

---

[3] Smith 2014.
[4] *Situationist International Anthology*: 14–21; Klein 2001: 309–42.

Luke's next stepping stone toward vaporwave involved the colonization of the planet Mars.

In 2010, a friend from high school, the artist Bronwyn Holloway-Smith, began a conceptual project called Pioneer City, involving a marketing campaign to sell real estate in a fictitious colony planned for the Red Planet. A temporary showroom was opened in downtown Wellington and a billboard went up, along with a website for registering interest. As a satire on the utopianism of real-estate advertising, Pioneer City drew an arc from the colonial history of Holloway-Smith and Rowell's hometown "pioneer city" (Lower Hutt), through contemporary housing developments, to tech billionaire Elon Musk's futuristic schemes to populate Mars. To underline the point, Pioneer City was to be situated on Mars's Utopia Planitia.

The next stage of the campaign was a promotional video. *Destination Pioneer City* (codirected by Simon Ward) was completed in early 2012. As curator Rob Garrett notes, the video mimics the "style and language of airport arrival videos, city tourism promotional films and residential development advertising."[5] Flyover CGI animation is employed, along with stock lifestyle photographs, while a relentlessly upbeat narration extols the colony's amenities—and keeping the sales pitch bubbling along is a synthesizer soundtrack composed by Luke, all pulsing beats, perky keyboard lines, and Vangelis-style swells. While envisioning the future as a cut-price infomercial, a certain pathos complicates Pioneer City's satire. Even the most flagrant advertising, Garrett remarks, plays on the genuine

---

[5] Quoted in Holloway-Smith n.d.

hopes and dreams that motivate consumers, including first homeowners and economic migrants.

The *Destination Pioneer City* soundtrack, while credited to Disasteradio, was the testing ground for Luke's vaporwave style. It presages Eyeliner in several respects. First, it relies on a limited musical palette. Roped in at short notice, Luke kept it simple, employing a single instrument, the 1990 Korg Wavestation keyboard, for which he had a virtual emulation on his computer. Faithful observation of advertising genre conventions was also key. Produced on the fly, the soundtrack comes across as genuinely cheap and cheerful. The video foreshadows Eyeliner's thematic interest in the utopianism of consumer advertising, too. *Destination Pioneer City* initially screened at festivals and galleries, later being made available on the in-flight entertainment system of the national carrier, Air New Zealand.

By this stage in Disasteradio's recording history, Luke's musical productions had become technically demanding: certain tracks on *Charisma* feature over forty instrumental layers. Between study, touring, and freelancing, the album had taken three years to complete. Although he had already started work on the follow-up that would become *Sweatshop* (2017), Luke acknowledges that frustration had set in. *Destination Pioneer City* turned out to be a liberating experiment.

> I realized I could take all the stuff that I'd written for Disasteradio—there were half-finished instrumentals—and use all those instruments, the Korg Wavestation stuff that I had discovered in *Pioneer City*, as a sort of self-contained unit . . . it could celebrate all these ad-hoc fast processes . . . have them

all played by the same plugin, so they all sounded in the same sound world, and I didn't have to labor over them as hard as I would for Disasteradio. I can just put it out.

A few months later, Eyeliner's debut, *High Fashion Mood Music*, was released on the label Crystal Magic Records as a CD–R and digital download.

Crystal Magic Records (CMR) was a small Bandcamp label founded by Fraser Austin, another New Zealand synthpop musician. Already, CMR had been venturing into vaporwave territory, with releases such as Power Nap's *No Worries* (2011) and RealPlayer 7's *REAL* (2012) having a corporate vibe and synthetic sound reminiscent of Ferraro's *Far Side Virtual*.[6] The label's artwork also looked back to the typefaces, screen icons, and other visual clichés of the early Internet, an interest Luke shared, having become "obsessed" with fake-marble desktop themes and default fonts like Times New Roman. He already knew everyone on CMR: Eyeliner and the label were a natural fit.

High Fashion Mood Music (*HFMM*) maintains the infomercial tone of *Destination Pioneer City* but also draws from adjacent musical areas. The liner notes mention "muzik [*sic*] library albums," for instance, referring to Muzak, a brand of background music for shops and offices, and library music, generic soundtracks recorded for licensing to television or advertising productions. Also referenced is "the late Innovative Communication catalog." Innovative Communication was

---

[6]Power Nap is an alias for Chris Cudby (Golden Axe), RealPlayer 7 for Fraser Austin.

founded by German musician Klaus Schulze in 1978 to release experimental electronic music. After Schulze's departure in 1983, the label moved into a kitschier line of new-age and smooth jazz: the "late catalog." *High Fashion Mood Music*'s cover is itself an homage to Innovative Communication's post-1983 house style of white backgrounds, stock photos, and italicized serif fonts.

The pared-back arrangement style was one clear point of difference from Disasteradio. The new artistic identity was another. Repurposed from an *HFMM* track title, Luke liked "Eyeliner" for various reasons. It suggested drawing a line around something, reframing and recontextualizing it, somewhat like a *détournement*. The name's camp connotations of putting on a mask or gender also appealed. Camp had been another topic of long-standing interest to Luke that Chris Tonelli had covered in his lectures. First analyzed by Susan Sontag, camp is an aesthetic sensibility that revels in exaggeration and artifice, either as a quality discovered in existing culture (often mass-produced kitsch) or to inform new works. "[The] essence of Camp is its love of the unnatural," Sontag writes.[7] "To perceive Camp in objects and persons is to understand Being-as-Playing-a-Role."[8] "Eyeliner" suited the album concept, too, each track title being conceived of as the name of a perfume. "I watched a lot of perfume and aftershave adverts while making it," Luke later said.[9]

---

[7] Sontag 1966: 275.
[8] Sontag 1966: 280.
[9] deliriously…daniel 2019: 48.

The album liner notes ply their own metafictional ironies, including quotes attributed to the artist behind Eyeliner: "'2012 finds me as a more complete person: running daily, exploring fine vegetarian cuisine, men's health and fashion, and the meaning of Real Love'—Luke Rowell." (The artist's actual lifestyle was lower budget than this might suggest.) Luke mastered the album with Computer Dreams in mind using "an acoustically efficient MP3 compression rate of 96 kilobytes per second." This technical note gently satirizes digital audiophile recordings, but it also expresses Luke's sincere interest in the archaeology of digital audio. Eyeliner's postironic odyssey thus begins.

High Fashion Mood Music was released on Bandcamp on July 11, 2012. By the end of the year, the album had been embraced in the budding vaporwave scene as a foundational work, being included with fourteen others on the first of many vaporwave "essentials" lists that would be posted on 4Chan and Reddit in the years to come. From here on, Eyeliner was in the canon. If Disasteradio's "Gravy Rainbow" had provided Luke's first online viral moment, this next would have more lasting ramifications. He had gotten in on the ground floor of a new musical style.

How did this come about? While *High Fashion Mood Music* certainly fit the bill, vaporwave did not exist as a named genre when the album was released. "Vaporwave" was not used as a tag on the album's original Bandcamp page, nor was Luke yet aware of the term. How did his side project on a relatively obscure New Zealand label gain the attention of this nascent Internet subculture? The answer, it turns out, involves the concurrent emergence of vaporwave itself across the networks of Web 2.0.

By mid-2012, the early vaporwave of Computer Dreams, Ferraro, and others had been circulating for up to two years. Their consolidation as examples of a new genre is generally credited to the article "Vaporwave and the Pop-Art of the Virtual Plaza" by Adam Harper, published by the UK music web magazine *Dummy* on July 12, 2012 (the day after *High Fashion Mood Music* was released on Bandcamp).[10]

Harper was one of several critics—including Mark Fisher and Simon Reynolds—who were writing about music on the nostalgia genre continuum. In 2010, Fisher spoke of these genres as signs of a cultural impasse,[11] while the following year Reynolds would characterize them as part of a twenty-first-century malaise he called "retromania" in his book of that title.[12] But Adam Harper (b.1986), younger than these veteran music writers, was fascinated by the ongoing expansion of the nostalgia continuum in the online underground.

New musical compounds, he argued in the *Dummy* article, were still bubbling up there. One of the most notable genres he dubbed "vaporwave." The musical period being reimagined was one point of difference. Where hypnagogic pop, for instance, looked back to the sounds of the 1970s and 1980s, vaporwave was focused on "material from the early 1990s onwards that can pass for contemporary."[13] The sources of inspiration were also unusual. Vaporwave tracks were like "chunk[s] of corporate mood music ... perfect for that infomercial, that menu screen, that in-flight safety video, that

---

[10] Harper 2012a.
[11] "Revenant Forms: The Meaning of Hauntology."
[12] Reynolds 2011.
[13] All quotes in the next three paragraphs are from Harper 2012a.

business park promotional video, that drinks reception in the lobby." Among the artists Harper identified with the embryonic style were James Ferraro, Computer Dreams, and INTERNET CLUB, along with Laserdisc Visions and 情報デスクVIRTUAL (both aliases for Ramona Langley).

In Harper's estimation, the oppressive implications of neoliberal capitalism were vaporwave's central concern. This theme was signaled by the artists' quasi-corporate aliases, album titles, and the music itself. In sampling or recreating a 1990s corporate sound, then looping, slowing, or glitching it, vaporwave conjured up an unsettling utopia where consumer fantasies had flooded all human consciousness:

> Global capitalism is nearly there. At the end of the world there will only be liquid advertisement and gaseous desire. Sublimated from our bodies, our untethered senses will endlessly ride escalators through pristine artificial environments, more and less than human, drugged-up and drugged down, catalysed, consuming and consumed by a relentlessly rich economy of sensory information, valued by the pixel. The Virtual Plaza welcomes you, and you will welcome it too.

Harper explained vaporwave's apparent ambivalence about capitalism (was it resisting or admiring?) using the post-Marxist concept of "accelerationism." The capitalist system, so the theory goes, should not be opposed but rather propelled ever faster into self-annihilation so that a better society can be born from the ashes.[14] Luxuriating in musical kitsch was

---

[14]Whelan 2020: 195–7.

accelerationist because it held up hyper-commercialized culture's hollowness for scrutiny, whether the artist is explicitly critical or not. An artist Harper interviewed for the article, Robin Burnett (INTERNET CLUB), seemed to confirm this view. Citing Debord, they explained their work as a *détournement* on stock music that sought to unmask the "false promises" of corporate culture.

In researching the article, Harper also consulted Burnett about recent user-generated tags attached to such music on the website LastFM. Burnett responded positively to the term "vaporwave."[15] Harper liked it, too. There was the apparent pun on vaporware (see Introduction), and he also recalled the phrase "all that is solid melts into air" from Karl Marx and Friedrich Engels's 1848 *Communist Manifesto*, describing capitalism's purported disintegrating effect on social cohesion and tradition.

News of "Vaporwave and the Pop-Art of the Virtual Plaza" spread fast online. It was recommended on the 4Chan /mu/ (i.e., music) discussion board, where the term "vaporwave" had started to be used only days earlier by another artist Harper interviewed, Ramona Langley. The concept seemed to click. Back in New Zealand, Harper's article was passed around Luke's networks, and he encountered the term "vaporwave" for the first time. "[Harper] was trying to define and point out a movement and he did that quite well," Luke observes. *High Fashion Mood Music*, in retrospect, seemed closely aligned, and

---

[15] The term's earliest known appearance was in an October 2011 blog post (Harper 2013b).

CMR added a "vaporwave" tag to the Bandcamp release page soon afterward.

It was another *Dummy* article by Adam Harper, "Isn't It Ironic?," published on August 28, 2012, that most likely brought *High Fashion Mood Music* to wider attention. Harper here brackets Eyeliner with the vaporwave artists he'd covered six weeks earlier. Being recognized by this critic, whose writings appeared in respected music magazines such as *The Wire*, was probably instrumental in Eyeliner being noticed and then adopted by the movement.

But what had led Harper to discover Eyeliner? Possibly that newly added Bandcamp "vaporwave" tag, although other New Zealand connections were also involved. It turns out that Harper subscribed to an experimental music blog, *Rose Quartz*, one of those previously aggregated into *Altered Zones*. *Rose Quartz* was run by a New Zealander, Richard MacFarlane, who'd previously blogged about Disasteradio and Crystal Magic. Harper recalls receiving news of *High Fashion Mood Music*'s release via *Rose Quartz*'s RSS feed. As it happens, the New Zealand blog had already covered many of the early vaporwave albums Harper later cited. He even credits their April 23, 2012, post about 情報デスクVIRTUAL to "[putting] me on to vaporwave in the first place."[16] Eyeliner's early profile thus got amplified through a series of Web 2.0 feedback loops in which local and global networks overlapped.

The "Virtual Plaza" article put vaporwave on the map. It neatly defined an underground music movement, packaging it with

---

[16] Email from Adam Harper, October 17, 2023.

theoretical interpretation and relevant subtexts, wrapped up with a catchy name. In retrospect, it was a bit too neat. Signs that Harper was expanding his thinking are evident in the "Isn't It Ironic?" article. Discussing *High Fashion Mood Music*, he frames the music's apparent ambivalence not through accelerationism but as a problem of irony. Harper notes that the "kitschy musical expressions" of Eyeliner seem, on the surface, to be asking audiences to listen ironically, to smirk at the emotional clichés of Muzak:

> But after a few listens, I'd gone in too deep—and Eyeliner had clearly gone to too much care and effort—for this musical experience for it to be a simple, cynical, irony-as-opposite affair. I began to see the appeal of the simple emotions and harmonies, and notice the cleverness of the musical constructions in (what you might call) their own right.[17]

He concludes that Eyeliner, James Ferraro, INTERNET CLUB, and others were exploring new conjunctions of irony and sincerity: "a continual testing and enlargement of the self, its faith and its aesthetic ideologies, across a distance that shifts with listening." *HFMM* was a work that challenged listeners to also pause and contemplate their reactions to capitalism's musical utopias, rather than give over to easy mockery.

Harper's next *Dummy* article on vaporwave, "Invest in Vaporwave Futures!" (July 29, 2013), consolidated this more expansive view. He began with a self-critique, acknowledging that his original "characterisation of vaporwave as a sarcastic,

---

[17] Harper 2012b.

satirical and insincere gesture probably went a little far."[18] There had been online pushback from artists too, with one of those he'd originally consulted, Robin Burnett, complaining on Twitter that their music had been reduced to "marxist plunderphonics." Harper accepted that vaporwave's ironic *détournement* of 1980s–1990s corporate music was counterbalanced by a sincere aesthetic response. "Vaporwave is a study in Utopianism," he concludes. The genre's inner postirony was now clearly in view.

The vaporwave subculture was well-established by the time "Invest in Vaporwave Futures!" came out. Key platforms in the early years included Tumblr, 4Chan, Soundcloud, and especially the r/vaporwave subreddit on the discussion site Reddit; Tinychat concerts live streamed from artists' houses also began early.[19] The scene's Internet profile was different from those of previous nostalgia genres. As Georgina Born and Christopher Haworth observe, rather than clustering around music blogs (hauntology) or label websites (hypnagogic pop, chillwave), the vaporwave subculture manifests as a dense network of user accounts on micro-blogging sites. "Vaporwave's online subculture," they conclude, "embodies the participatory, user-generated content ethos of 'web 2.0.'"[20]

By late 2012, this subculture had already got down to the business of sorting out the classic vaporwave albums. The first such canon appeared in November, produced by users of the 4Chan /mu/ board. Following in 4Chan tradition, */mu/*

---

[18] Harper 2013a; cf. Killeen 2018: 631.
[19] Galil 2013.
[20] Born and Haworth 2018: 634.

VAPORWAVE ESSENTIALS is a Topsters-style mosaic chart of album covers.[21] It features many albums mentioned in "Virtual Plaza," including releases that would soon gain prominence, such as Daniel Lopatin's *Chuck Person's Eccojams Vol. 1* (2010) and Macintosh Plus's *Floral Shoppe* (2011); *High Fashion Mood Music* was there too. Updated charts would appear over coming years.[22]

Such a heightened sense of self-awareness is another one of vaporwave's traits. "The *condition of being a genre* ... appears to be a primary, ironic, and meta-reflexive concern," Born and Haworth note.[23] Even vaporwave's claim to being a bona-fide music genre at all was playfully debated. As early as February 2013, for instance, some were declaring that "vaporwave is dead" due to growing outside attention, such as *Floral Shoppe* being reviewed by prominent YouTuber Anthony Fantano.[24] "Vaporwave is dead" quickly became a popular meme that ironically mocked the baby boomer proverb "rock is dead,"[25] the subculture getting there first. The genre thus proved to be both dead and alive.[26] As artists pushed the style in different directions, vaporwave subgenre names were coined that had a similar postironic flavor. Amusing in marking out tiny stylistic variations, they also reveal what has genuinely caught the imagination of artists and fans, whether shopping-mall culture

---

[21] Girls Blood 2012.
[22] Kilby 2017.
[23] Born and Haworth 2018: 636, original emphasis.
[24] Fantano 2012.
[25] Dettmar 2013: 26–8.
[26] Beauchamp 2016.

(mallsoft), dreamy ambience (hypnagogic drift), or drugged-out grooves (future funk).

Back in Wellington, Luke watched the vaporwave scene unfold and dived in himself. He reckons being among the first twenty subscribers to the r/vaporwave subreddit and attended early SPF420 online festivals. Vaporwave appealed on multiple levels. There was the DIY curatorship involved, albums drawing together samples of forgotten music, and fans constructing playlists and canons. "I was in there trying to post a lot of proto vaporwave," Luke remembers of r/vaporwave. "What I was seeing as vaporwave, the genesis of these modes." There was also the open-source ethos, new albums being freely shared through Bandcamp, MediaFire, and other platforms.

Nor was Luke the only New Zealander involved. Crystal Magic Records released more from RealPlayer 7 and Power Nap, along with vaporwave by other local artists, Daif and Splash Club 7. "We had a pretty good community for a while there . . . with CMR," Luke remembers. "A lot of word of mouth, sharing cool images or weird EPs . . . coming up with stupid subgenres." Adam Harper later described CMR vaporwave as an example of "convergent evolution."[27] New Zealand artists seemed to have arrived at the genre alongside and simultaneously with others. Web 2.0 was collapsing not only the geographic distance that had previously stymied many New Zealand musicians but also cultural distance. The CMR artists and *Rose Quartz* writers were among those stirring the crucible of a new global style as it was born.

---

[27] Harper 2013c; cf. 2013a.

Luke remained plugged into the vaporwave world, even while working primarily on new Disasteradio tracks. But offline factors also nudged him further toward Eyeliner. In October 2012, he injured his knee at a gig, and Disasteradio went on hold as a live act. The six-month rehabilitation gave him the opportunity to ponder Eyeliner further. He even devised a real-world version to fulfill some bookings. Seated at a laptop in suit and tie, Luke performed what he describes as "this kind of Victor Borge prop humor live show," the gigs providing a sandpit for further developing the Eyeliner persona.

Life cycle changes were also taking effect. Those in Luke's social circles had, like him, reached the end of their twenties, and many were looking for more economic stability. The bohemian scene he'd been part of in Wellington for ten years began to fray. A decline in Wellington's live music scene contributed, too, with the post-2008 Global Financial Crisis (GFC) recession and costly new earthquake-strengthening regulations dimming the capital city's vibrancy. New Zealand's then prime minister, John Key, went so far as to declare Wellington "a dying city."[28] Two key music venues closed permanently in mid-2014, with others to follow.[29] In this context, the Internet-based music of Eyeliner became more appealing.

Luke and his wife Chris Hroch also separated around the time of the accident. They'd been together since the early Disasteradio days. Luke's musical response to the breakup was the Disasteradio instrumental EP *Electric Blanket*, released by CMR in April 2013, after which there would be no more

---

[28] Quoted in Stahl 2018: 125.
[29] Stahl 2018.

Disasteradio releases for four years. Even after his knee came right, Luke played only twenty shows for the whole of 2013 and 2014. His next musical step was another Eyeliner album, released by CMR in November 2013.

Sporting Fraser Austin's sleek cover artwork—a framed eye peering through a circular lens into a square of virtual blue sky—*LARP of Luxury* refines the Eyeliner aesthetic. Composed once more using the virtual Korg Wavestation, the album's sonic polish befits the overarching concept of a live-action roleplay (LARP) of luxury: "The roleplay of desire, the act of fashion, a post-consumer social-network profile of an artist faking comfort," as the press release puts it. The nine tracks are mostly named after brands from the 1990s–2000s era such as Nespresso, iPod Shuffle, and The North Face, luxurious in the sense of decent quality, rather than having astronomical price tags. Even if one is not born in the true lap of luxury, the album title puns, one can at least enjoy the LARP of mass comforts.

Eyeliner again received kudos from Adam Harper, who ranked *LARP of Luxury* third best vaporwave album of 2013, also citing it in *The Wire*.[30] The album consolidated several key aspects of Eyeliner's sensibility in the lead-up to *BUY NOW*. First, the clean synthetic sound. Pristine sonics, as heard on *Far Side Virtual*, had been part of vaporwave from the start, but the impact of *Floral Shoppe* and the relative ease of emulating its eccojams approach had pushed the chopped-and-screwed style to the forefront of the genre.[31] Eyeliner instead took the

---

[30] Harper 2013c, 2014.
[31] Chopping-and-screwing was a technique developed in the Houston (Texas) hip-hop scene (Whelan 2020: 194).

Ferraro-inspired vaporwave path less traveled. Along with albums by Pyravid, LensCorp™ International, and PrismCorp Virtual Enterprises (Ramona Langley again), Eyeliner albums are often filed into the subgenre utopian virtual.[32] Referencing *Far Side Virtual*, the name draws an analogy between 1990s advertising dreamworlds and the pristine surfaces of digitally generated music.

Sample-free original composition was another defining Eyeliner quality represented on the album. Eyeliner's *détournement* is to appropriate styles rather than existing recordings. This approach is also unusual for vaporwave, but Luke was already accustomed to composing original music for Disasteradio—and he had another incentive, too. Back in 2008, he had become involved with the Creative Freedom Foundation (CFF), set up by Bronwyn Holloway-Smith and her husband Matt Holloway to advocate for copyright reform. Most famously, CFF organized the 2009 New Zealand Internet Blackout to protest efforts by the entertainment industry to make local ISPs liable for unauthorized file-sharing by their customers. "We were under international scrutiny," Luke recalls. "If I was caught sampling other people's music, we would be delegitimizing CFF's actions." Thereafter, he had generally avoided the use of samples.

LARP of Luxury also reaffirmed key aspects of the Eyeliner persona. Luke bucked the artist-anonymity trend in vaporwave from the start, being open that he was the artist behind Eyeliner. Yet the Eyeliner persona is significantly different from Disasteradio. In a 2015 interview, he described Disasteradio as a

---

[32] Chennington 2019.

vehicle for his "essential self," a channel for expressing personal views; Eyeliner, by contrast, was "pretending."[33] The roleplay afforded its own conceptual possibilities. As suggested by the *HFMM* liner notes (see above), for instance, the Eyeliner role satirizes "Brand You" self-marketing concepts, the notion of the freelancer as "independent owner and manager of her so-called human capital."[34] It brings the idea that creative workers are themselves products for sale into the vaporwave frame. (The Eyeliner "character" is discussed further in Chapter 3.)

Tying these conceptual strands together is one of Luke's favorite epigrams, picked up from Chris Tonelli's lectures: "Camp is the lie that tells the truth." Not only is Eyeliner a campy roleplay: Luke considers vaporwave itself as a kind of "lie that tells the truth."[35] On the one hand, vaporwave's fake soundtrack exposes consumer advertising's own deceptions for what they are. On the other, vaporwave liberates such music from its original function. "Why not then make a version of it that doesn't have that exploitation built into it?" he asks. "Inoculate it from capitalism." The celebratory quality of Eyeliner's music stems from this positive impulse toward vaporwave's sources.

Luke's other favorite aphorism that helps define vaporwave is "Capitalism imagining its own eternity."[36] This phrase takes us back to the 1990s, a decade when such thinking was topical. The era really begins with the fall of the Berlin Wall in 1989 and the subsequent collapse of communism in Russia and Eastern Europe, following which the philosopher Francis Fukuyama

---

[33] Arnold 2015.
[34] Konstantinou 2016: 223.
[35] Yabsley and Davoren-Britton 2014; Arnold 2015; deliriously…daniel 2019: 49.
[36] Thomas 2017.

famously declared the triumph of neoliberal capitalism and "the end of history." The next fifteen years were economic boom times in the West. The GDP of countries such as New Zealand grew steadily; technological optimism reigned. Capitalism could plausibly be imagined as lasting indefinitely. "In New Zealand . . . it seemed like everyone was doing well," Luke remembers.

> And then something happened. I don't know what it was. But everyone I talk to seems like, "Everyone was comfy in the mid-nineties." . . . If we are looking for a time, a place that is frozen in time, it's when it seemed like my parents could afford stuff for the first time in their lives. They rebuilt their house, and we were living in our own bedrooms. Things seemed kind of easy. But after the GFC, I was living in a draughty loft space above the panel beaters, with spray paint fumes coming through the floor. I wasn't in any position to lose anything.

The 2008 Global Financial Crisis had the most impact on the millennial generation that includes Luke and other musicians who invented vaporwave. More than other generations, the ensuing recession affected millennials' ability to establish careers, save to buy a family home, and otherwise progress their lives.[37] It also dispelled any sense of eternal prosperity they might have grown up with.

In 2014, around the time he started work on *BUY NOW*, Luke mused upon these connections for the podcast *Genre Cult*. "[Is vaporwave] generation Y . . . kind of realizing that the dream

---

[37] Duffy 2021: 34.

we were shown in the nineties is not actually true and sort of making it true, but then showing it to be false," he wondered. "I don't think there's any other musical movement that has approached this ambiguity."[38] Post-GFC, millennials like himself might look back fondly to the utopias they soaked up as children of the 1990s. They might also ponder the economic system that oversaw the greatest destruction of new wealth since the 1930s Depression. The ironies were complex in New Zealand. In 2008, the country elected John Key as their prime minister, a former "state-house kid" who'd risen to become head of global foreign exchange at Merrill Lynch, one of the US firms later blamed for the GFC, before turning to politics. Key helped steer New Zealand through the recession and was twice re-elected.

In 2014, as he began working on *LARP of Luxury*'s follow-up, something else was on Luke's mind too. He had started noticing social media posts by listeners appreciative of Eyeliner, even finding the music therapeutic. Some fans sent personal messages: "Emails from people saying, 'I listened to this in a period of my life that was challenging.'" Such responses were humbling. They also changed Luke's perspective on what had originally been a musical side-project. "It's what gave *BUY NOW* its intricacy, its attention to detail, and layering," he recalls. "I felt the responsibility to get it right and provide more of a deep listening experience." Making the album found him at a crossroads: "*BUY NOW* was a sort of culmination of [the] second act in my life leading into my thirties."

---

[38] Yabsley and Davoren-Britton 2014.

3 Virtual LARPing in the Musical Past

The making of an album most readily calls to mind the recording studio—that almost mythical place where personalities sizzle, creative lightning strikes, and musical art is brought forth into the world. *BUY NOW* exemplifies a new paradigm for the twenty-first century: the artist alone with their computer.

If, in recent years, the Internet has changed how music genres might be constituted, computer technology has long been transforming music production and composition. From the incorporation of microprocessors in synthesizers and drum machines in the 1970s through to the 64-bit software applications of today, technology has dramatically expanded artists' creative palettes. In this new context, understanding the making of an album means investigating the tools involved and, equally, grasping the decisions behind and implications of their use. These matters are especially important with an artist such as Luke, for whom technology has always held a fascination.

This chapter explores how *BUY NOW* was conceptualized and practically realized, including real-world influences on the creative process. The first two Eyeliner albums looked back to the sound world of the Korg Wavestation. For his next vaporwave statement, Luke set the controls for a new musical constellation.

Luke has a long-held belief in the democratic potential of computers. As he told Ian Jorgenson in 2004, "I love the utopian idea of technology being a system for universal good (however wrong I may be)."[1] According to this philosophy, anybody with a computer has the tools necessary to compose music; they render investments in time and money to acquire instruments, manual dexterity, and theoretical knowledge largely unnecessary. Hence Luke's preferred description of himself as a "computer musician" rather than an "electronic musician," because of the latter's less democratic connotations of mastery over expensive equipment.

From the early Disasteradio years, Luke's main creative tool had been Jeskola Buzz. It's a powerful software application, but after completing *Visions* in 2007, he was ready to move on. He was coming up against Buzz's technical limitations and chose to switch to the digital audio workstation Nuendo. By this stage, digital audio workstations (DAWs) were well-established as the standard application for recording, manipulating, and mixing audio files. Most—including Nuendo—also had sampling and MIDI sequencing capabilities.[2] The first DAWs had been constrained by the native processing power of 1990s-era PCs. High-end examples such as Pro Tools required their own microprocessor cards for real-time previewing of mixes and signal processing. But a decade on, PC hardware

---
[1] Blink 2004: 30.
[2] Burgess 2014: 134–46.

had advanced, and a DAW such as Nuendo could be run using off-the-shelf systems.

Released in 2000 by the German music software company Steinberg, Nuendo was derived from their earlier and still popular DAW, Cubase. Its added video-editing functions were appealing for Luke given the filmmaking going on at Skyranch. Nuendo was also his gateway into MIDI. Musical Instrument Digital Interface is an open-source technical standard developed in the early 1980s to enable synthesizers, sequencers, and other electronic equipment to communicate. Instructions relating to musical notes' pitch, timing, and other parameters can thus be sent from one device to another, triggering sounds. MIDI soon became a standard file format. The first version of Cubase (released in 1989) was essentially a MIDI sequencer, with sound samples being triggered according to MIDI patterns programmed by the user.

Shifting from Buzz's tracker system to Nuendo's MIDI approach appealed to Luke for the greater level of compositional nuance it provided. Where Buzz can specify musical instructions to the level of one-eighth of a quarter-note beat, MIDI can slice up a quarter-note 480 times.[3] Advances in DAW plug-in technology were another attraction. Plug-ins are self-contained software components that can be added (i.e., plugged in) to a DAW to provide new functions. The earliest plug-ins offered compression, equalization, and other standard studio effects, but in 1999 there was a major advance when Steinberg expanded its Virtual Studio Technology (VST) protocol. This expansion, Peter Manning

---

[3] Manning 2013: 277.

explains, "allowed plug-ins that generated instrumental voices to be directly controlled by MIDI."[4] VSTi plug-ins ("i" stands for "instrument") were soon released that emulated the circuitry and firmware of older synthesizers. Playing MIDI compositions back through these virtual synthesizers produces uncannily realistic simulations of gear which, in the twenty-first century, might be difficult to obtain. VSTi technology was a game changer for Luke. "My shift from tracker software to MIDI and the VST plugins was when the analog emulation stuff became quite good and quite affordable," he remarks. "I realized I could make more authentic synthpop using these recreations of vintage synths."

Luke taught himself MIDI composition on the Nuendo DAW while producing Disasteradio's *Charisma* (another reason why producing the album took three years). The making of *High Fashion Mood Music* and *LARP of Luxury* involved further upskilling, but by the time he began working on *BUY NOW*, Luke was well-versed. He had also acquired his latest PC, a hand-me-down from Simon Ward featuring an Intel Core i5 CPU for smoother and faster processing. The latest MIDI-VSTi adventure awaited.

Slap bass, Korg M1, and LinnDrum—these three musical ingredients lie at the heart of *BUY NOW*. The initial inspiration for this prescription was romance. Midway through 2013, Luke began a relationship with jeweler-designer Chloe Rose Taylor, and an especially memorable part of their courtship was watching old TV shows together, with one standout

---

[4] Manning 2013: 399.

example: "We just sat around and watched *Seinfeld* for months and months," Luke recalls. Running for nine seasons from 1989, this vehicle for American comedian Jerry Seinfeld is the very epitome of 1990s ironic humor. The sitcom also features the famous slap bass theme by Jonathan Wolff. Binge viewing of *Seinfeld* led Luke to revive an unrealized concept. "Before I even started," he told Zac Arnold in 2015, "I was considering having an album where every song had slap bass on it."[5]

BUY NOW's second primary ingredient now came into view. Wolff had played *Seinfeld*'s hyperactive basslines not on an actual instrument but by editing together samples of slap bass patches (instrumental voices) from different synthesizer keyboards. Prominent among these was the Korg M1's Slap Bass preset.[6]

The M1 workstation, released by the Japanese electronics company Korg in 1988, is said to be the best-selling synthesizer of all time.[7] The keyboard includes an eight-track MIDI sequencer, numerous onboard effects, and many iconic patches. Luke had long used and appreciated Korg gear, and he already had the Korg Legacy Collection, a VSTi with emulations of the Wavestation and M1. Previous Eyeliner albums were based around the Wavestation and the idea of now exploring the sound world of the M1 took hold.

One more ingredient was needed though. In Luke's view, the Korg M1's drum patches are "a little bit too bright and too hyped." The solution was LinnDrum, a drum machine released

---

[5] Arnold 2015.
[6] Emmerling 2020.
[7] Vail 2002.

in 1982 and used for many famous recordings. Luke did not have access to an actual unit, but years earlier had acquired a set of LinnDrum samples. Loading these into a generic VSTi drum-machine plug-in (Linplug RMIV) he could create a virtual LinnDrum drumkit for the album.

Why slap bass, Korg M1, and LinnDrum? The short answer is that all are emblematic of the popular music soundscape of vaporwave's period of musical reimagining, with the M1 being a precise lodestone for the late 1980s to early 1990s era. The instrumental threesome also has strong associations with the fourth cardinal point on *BUY NOW*'s musical compass: R&B, particularly the combination of shuffle rhythm, jazzy chords, and funk syncopation prevalent in the 1980s. Slap bass is, by definition, a funk technique, while LinnDrum helped usher in a quantized swing-shuffle feel.[8] Although the Korg M1 is not so specifically connected with R&B, such digital keyboards were central to the modernization of the genre in this period.

R&B had come into the frame soon after Luke started work on *BUY NOW*. "The first two albums, I shot from the hip," he later told Zac Arnold. "But with *BUY NOW*, I was thinking about vaporware . . . about the way it sounded and trying to respond to it in my own way."[9] Use of chopped-and-screwed R&B samples had become widespread in vaporwave since 2012. *Floral Shoppe* features samples from Diana Ross, Anita Baker, and Sade tracks, among others, and numerous artists had followed suit. Luke's response with *BUY NOW* was to evoke vaporwave's R&B influence by composing all-original versions.

---

[8] LeRoy 2023: 140.
[9] Arnold 2015.

BUY NOW was also an opportunity for Luke to reconnect body with music and up his funk skills generally. The 2012 knee injury had required a long recovery, complicated by a lingering bout of mononucleosis (glandular fever). Fully back on his feet in early 2014, he could revert to his preferred method of composing music at a standing desk. *BUY NOW* became a way to find his groove again.

BUY NOW's three primary ingredients were also ripe for postironic interpretation. Take slap bass. This style involves introducing percussive sounds into electric bass guitar parts by "slapping," striking the strings against the fretboard with a knuckle, and "popping," pulling and releasing strings to snap back. Invented by Larry Graham, the original bassist for Sly and the Family Stone, the technique became an essential part of the funk bass toolkit during the 1970s, with renowned stylists including Louis Johnson (Brothers Johnson), Bernard Edwards (Chic), and Marcus Miller. While making *BUY NOW*, Luke became particularly enamored of Freddie Washington's propulsive playing on Patrice Rushen's 1982 R&B single "Forget Me Nots" (later sampled for Will Smith's 1997 hit "Men in Black"). The track captures the style's essence. "Slap bass is the fun guy that shows at the party," Luke comments. "Doing cool things and crazy stuff."

Yet slap bass's sheer overexposure—coupled with its comedic associations—has also given rise to perceptions of kitsch. The style's potential for becoming a fashionable cliché was perceived early on. Donald Fagen and Walter Becker, for example, were apparently reluctant to feature slap on Steely Dan's *Aja* (1977), "[m]ainly because at that time slapping was just becoming popular and it was on a lot of records," bassist Chuck Rainey recalled in 1999.[10] During the 1980s, slap bass spread into synthpop and rock, and by the 2000s *Bass Player* magazine was referring to slap as a "now-ubiquitous technique" of which players might well "consciously steer clear."[11] Slap's humorous potential, the quirky vocal-like qualities exploited by *Seinfeld*, also fueled suspicions of musical fooling around. Luke was aware of the ambiguities. "A bit funny . . . sort of hokey . . . a little bit naff," he told Zac Arnold in 2015.[12] Slap, in other words, was a style that could be regarded both sincerely and ironically.

The Korg M1 held postironic potential for similar reasons. One of the original controversies provoked by the use of synthesizers in the 1980s related to "timbral conformity." As Andrew Goodwin explains, "many drum machines and synthesizers come with built-in factory sounds (presets) that are either unalterable or that make changing the sounds . . . so difficult that only the most dedicated users even bother to try."[13] Conformity bred monotony. A classic example is the Yamaha DX7's E.PIANO 1 preset, so fashionable that in 1986 it ended up being featured on 39 percent of *Billboard* Hot 100 #1 singles and 61 percent of R&B #1s.[14] According to a 1995 *Keyboard* magazine article, "20 Sounds That Must Die!," such preset patches embody a paradox: "popular because they're so

---

[10] *Steely Dan—Aja: Classic Albums.*
[11] Leslie 2007: 31.
[12] Arnold 2015.
[13] Goodwin 1992: 84.
[14] Lavengood 2019: 74.

cool, but uncool because they're so popular."[15] The magazine demanded a death sentence for "DX7 *anything*."

The Korg M1 has a similar legacy of wide use, including by Depeche Mode, the Cure, Madonna, Pet Shop Boys, and the KLF. By 1995, *Keyboard* reckoned, saturation point had been reached for at least five M1 presets: PanFlute, PanMallet, Lore, Pole, and MagicOrgan. PanFlute and similar patches were also redolent of new-age music, a genre widely discredited as kitsch at the time.[16]

The Korg M1, however, has never quite rivalled the DX7's reputation for cheesiness. It includes a palette of 244 onboard presets[17] (almost double that of the Yamaha), with over 2,000 others available through ROM expansion cards. The M1 patches were also easier to customize, partly because they used digital sampling technology. From a postironic perspective then, the Korg affords a more subtle play between irony and sincerity, especially in the hands of a connoisseur such as Luke. "Korg stuff is beautifully pocketed together," he observes. "If you keep stacking it over itself, it doesn't really begin to be too harsh or too mellow—or too retro . . . you can hear personality in it . . . a certain amount of camp."

LinnDrum offered a final balancing of the scales. Again, this drum machine was heavily used in the 1980s, including by Frankie Goes to Hollywood, Madonna, Womack & Womack, Billy Idol, and Miami Sound Machine. This heavy use has certainly inspired a few detractors. Famed engineer and

---

[15] Battino 1995: 65.
[16] Hibbett 2010.
[17] These consist of 100 basic patches, 100 combination patches, and 44 drum and percussion sounds.

hardcore musician, the late Steve Albini, for instance, referred to LinnDrum as part of the 1980s "bestiary of shit sound."[18] Yet its reputation has held up in other quarters. Prince is known for his innovative use of LinnDrum and its predecessor, the Linn LM-1.[19] A long-time fan of Prince's work, Luke praises the drum machine's sonic balance: "It's in the right zone of being not too much and not too little, not too punchy and not too mellow."

In combination, slap bass, Korg M1, and LinnDrum provide a rich vaporwave palette. Laden with period associations, they also invite the listener to ponder whether they're hearing loving homage or ironic study—or both.

To boot up a VSTi emulation of an old synthesizer is to step into a kind of virtual musical time machine. Even their onscreen appearance can imitate the textured surface, complete with logos, physical knobs, and other controls, of the original device. To operate such plug-ins becomes a kind of roleplay in itself and, in Luke's case, adds new layers to the Eyeliner roleplay already going on.

Tightly defining what virtual instruments will be used is crucial. "Eyeliner uses one ROMpler[20] VST plugin per album," Luke explained in a 2017 Reddit r/makingvaporwave guest post.

> Computers are great at producing whatever the heck you want but keep in mind if we want to pastiche a certain period or

---

[18] Posting at: https://bsky.app/profile/electricalwsop.bsky.social/post/3k6gede3ji72g (accessed September 3, 2023).
[19] LeRoy 2023: 145, 152–57.
[20] ROMplers are synthesizers like the Korg M1 that rely on digital audio samples stored on ROM.

approach, there are restrictions involved . . . these might have been having a studio with only a Wavestation and a sampler, or an M1 and a DX7, that sort of thing. This approach can make for some fun composition experiments—like pretend you've "borrowed" a Linndrum for the week off your buddy, and only use those samples for a week.[21]

What is the impetus behind this "pretending"? "It's not about nostalgia," Luke clarified for me in 2022, "but . . . about playing at an 'authenticity' . . . a construction." VSTi technology becomes a means (to riff on an Eyeliner album title) of virtual LARPing in the musical past. Crucially, he envisages such LARPing in terms of a specific "character." Rather than a producer with a gear-filled studio at their fingertips, Eyeliner is a lone journeyman: "some crank in a bedroom with a Korg M1 and an Atari ST." Compared with the flamboyant alter egos of stars like David Bowie or Eminem, there's something suitably postironic about roleplaying the humble "anonymous craftsmen" (as Adam Harper refers to them) of cut-price production music.[22]

A narrow musical prescription not only helps Luke to stay "in character." It mitigates certain pitfalls that he perceives in having the freedom to now range through the sounds of music history using computers. While Luke himself revels in such "contempt for time," overproduction is a risk. "You can hear records where they've sort of nervously put too many instruments over everything, and it's just too much," he

---

[21] Rowell 2017.
[22] Harper 2012a.

comments. Eyeliner's approach ("one ROMpler VST plugin per album") keeps things in focus.

The same discipline applies to any music listening in his downtime, which Luke regards as a form of album research. With *BUY NOW*, he repeatedly consulted key material from the genres and periods of interest: R&B 12" mixes, Jim Andron's 1992 CD-i Tetris game soundtrack, TV composer Mike Post's *Inventions from the Blue Line* (1994), German new-age group Cusco's *Apurimac II* (1994), and his vaporwave gold-standard, *Far Side Virtual*. Avoiding more recent music releases was crucial. "I don't want to ruin what I'm metabolizing," he states. "Just always be sticking with my period."

BUY NOW's diversity—the range of types of commercial music it explores—is a notable departure from previous Eyeliner albums. Where *LARP of Luxury* focuses primarily on brand advertising, for instance, individual tracks on *BUY NOW* can be regarded as studies in hold music, television themes and incidental scores, advertising, elevator music, Japanese anime soundtracks, genres such as new age, and more. Luke wanted to create a more "impressionistic," less "showy," take on vaporwave.

In its way, *BUY NOW*'s eclecticism reflects the evolution of commercial music during vaporwave's key period. The 1980s–1990s were not simply a golden age of consumerism; they represented a tipping point for popular music's integration with consumer culture. Music had been used in advertising long before the 1980s of course. But as Timothy Taylor explains, this decade saw advertisers pivot away from jingles toward licensing popular songs, either 1960s hits (appealing to baby boomers) or the latest hip sounds (for youth markets).[23] Familiar songs helped define the lifestyle associations that companies wanted their brands to project, and there was always the cheaper option of creating soundalikes, perhaps employing name performing-artists who needed the work. MTV accelerated the change. Music videos increased popular artists' exposure, making them ever more appealing to commercial interests. The MTV style of fast-paced editing over pop songs also crept into advertising, television shows, and movies. Another shift occurred in programmed background music for shops and malls. Traditional-style Muzak (syrupy renditions of old songs) was being supplanted by "foreground music": contemporary hits compiled for the specific market segments that retailers wanted to appeal to.[24] Commercial opportunities flowed the other way too, as artists began to realize the benefits of cross-media marketing and being associated with desirable products. "Selling out" was losing its stigma, even being considered hip.[25] By the 2000s, popular music's alliance with consumerism had gone full spectrum.

BUY NOW scans the state of play during the late-1980s to 1990s transition period. Vaporwave's sweet spot happens to be a time when the cracks between popular music and consumerism still showed, when the soundalike kitsch was still genuinely itself. The period just precedes the present epoch when, as Timothy Taylor puts it, there is "no longer a

---

[23] Taylor 2012: 165–204.
[24] Lanza 1994: 219–20.
[25] Klein 2001: 72; Taylor 2012: 207, 228.

meaningful distinction to be made between 'popular music' and 'advertising music.'"[26]

BUY NOW's widening field of vision was also stimulated by what was happening in Luke's freelance career. As he began working on the album in 2014, his workaday reality was starting to resemble the Eyeliner roleplay. Luke had done occasional advertising work over the years, composing Disasteradio-style synthpop for several commercials, such as for Samsung New Zealand's K5 MP3 players (2006) and an Australian tourism web series (2008).[27] Freelancing picked up markedly in 2013 though, as Luke looked to support himself while recuperating. He took on a variety of soundtrack and sound-design contracts, often creating musical pastiches with a chiptune vibe. A series of significant contracts came via Resn, a Wellington creative agency specializing in web campaigns and digital interactives. Like Peter Jackson's Weta, but on a smaller scale, Resn had leveraged new global data infrastructure and New Zealand's low cost-overheads to secure international clients, collaborating with renowned US agencies such as Wieden+Kennedy. Among the major brands on whose campaigns Luke worked were Gap, Kentucky Fried Chicken, Rubbermaid, and Belvita. Thus, at the same time as crafting Eyeliner's postironic take on commercial music, Luke was also being paid to produce the real thing. "It allowed me to put a totally authentic hat on," he remembers.

---

[26] Taylor 2012: 229.
[27] Curriculum Vitae (2019), Luke Rowell Collection.

The timeframes were so quick that I had to get better at what I was doing... It did lend itself to feeling like I was within the context of what I was pointing at [with Eyeliner]. Going from doing sound effects for an ad campaign, closing that session, and then opening what I was working on for *BUY NOW*... I got confidence from that.

Being "on the inside" provided real-world insights into creative briefs, agency workflows, and the various jobs a freelance producer might take. The work also raised the bar for Luke's appreciation of the care that went into commercial production. Compared with the quick turnarounds of the first Eyeliner albums, *BUY NOW* took far more time. It was the turning point when Luke's vaporwave side project became his main project.

A new level of depth and complexity is evident throughout *BUY NOW*. The VSTi presets used across the album provide one measure of this. *BUY NOW* uses a total of eighty-one different Korg M1 patches, twenty-four percussion patches, and seven further instruments from other VSTi plug-ins, as well as various sound effects samples. Very few patches are used on more than one of the album's eleven tracks, Luke crafting specific sound worlds for each. The most common preset is Slap'n'Thump, a version of the original *Seinfeld* M1 Slap Bass patch. But even so, Luke generally combines Slap'n'Thump with other bass patches to create timbral variation, with twelve others being used across the album.

More granular nuances are incorporated, too. These include adjustments to MIDI note velocity settings (how hard a note is played), which is how the realism of programmed Slap Bass is achieved. Many patches used on *BUY NOW* are also modified "combis." These combine two or more single-voice patches ("progs"), whether layering them together, assigning them different pitch zones, or programming them with a "velocity switch" to swap between patches according to how soft or hard notes are played. So, while *BUY NOW* has consistent ingredients at its core, these are richly varied throughout.

Luke's freelancing work also seems to have pushed *BUY NOW* across a new threshold of postirony. A sincerity of purpose permeates the album: the Eyeliner "character" clearly wants their clients to love his work. The album thus exhibits an insider's appreciation for the unseen labor of commercial music creatives; it pays proper respect to these "anonymous craftsmen."

BUY NOW is nonetheless still loaded with what Luke refers to as ironic "signposts" or "winks." These side comments, as will be explored in Chapter 4, might refer to the choice of a patch or a sample, or the characteristics of a melody or arrangement, a track's title often providing the cue for an ironic reading. Such "winks" operate as a stimulus for listeners to ponder commercial music's means and ends and appreciate its camp dimensions. Knowing that vaporwave fans had been listening so closely to Eyeliner also upped the stakes. Overall, *BUY NOW*'s "winks" tend to be more subtle than on previous albums: Luke was becoming mindful not to salt the music with too much sarcasm.

Work on *BUY NOW* began in early 2014. Some tracks drew from Luke's existing pool of sketches, while others were fresh compositions. Getting musical ideas into the computer happened in various ways. A traditional MIDI controller—a keyboard that converts played notes into data—was used for at least one track ("Private Hospital"). Mostly though, notes were input directly using the Korg VSTi's onscreen piano keyboard. Another type of software also came into play: MIDI generators.

MIDI generators are software applications that automate music composition and arrangement processes. Luke has long been a fan: they are another way that computers can help those who have musical ideas but not necessarily the training to realize them. He employed several on *BUY NOW*. Lending a distinctive flavor to much of the album is ChordSpace, a freeware plug-in released in 2005. It generates tetrachords (triads with a sixth or seventh added) and their various extensions, according to jazz theory. A graphic interface is used, with a tonic key at the center, surrounded by hexagons representing related chords and their potential substitutes. Pointing and clicking with a mouse plays the chords and generates MIDI data in the DAW sequencer. ChordSpace enables the user to try out possibilities by ear and find what flavor of jazz harmony sounds "right," without ever needing to understand jazz theory. The resulting MIDI can be tinkered with afterward in the sequencer.

For *BUY NOW*, Luke used ChordSpace to summon up the jazzy flavor of 1980s R&B, whether associated with crossover/smooth-jazz artists such as Patrice Rushen, George Benson, or Kenny G or as found on recordings by the likes of Alexander O'Neal or Whitney Houston. The results are evident across the album. Many tracks' tonic chords are altered to major or minor sevenths, their progressions filled with sixths and ninths. Unaltered major or minor chords are rare. But, as with many of the sources of inspiration, the album's "jazziness" is essentially a light seasoning sprinkled over straightforward chord sequences.

A more sophisticated MIDI generator, Band-in-a-Box, helped create a basic skeleton for several tracks. Predating generative AI by decades, the first version of Band-in-a-Box was released in 1990 by PG Music. Users set basic criteria—key, a few chords, tempo, and musical style (which has thousands of permutations)—and the software then generates a melody, chord progression, song structure, and instrumental arrangement. The algorithms are complex enough that identical inputs will generate different results each time. Band-in-a-Box provided Luke with basic MIDI for two tracks ("Payphone," "Windchimes"), which he then extensively reworked in Nuendo.

MIDI generators are a good example of the human-computer collaboration involved in Luke's music. The practice goes beyond mere practical convenience though. These tools involve what Luke describes as "established languages," which add further layers of verisimilitude and thematic depth to Eyeliner's period roleplay—and provide further ways to understand the broader meaning of *BUY NOW*.

Synthesizers, drum machines, and MIDI generators, like traditional music instruments, make specific "affordances" (sets of potential actions) available to users through their design. It is such affordances that give rise to Luke's sense of them having "established languages."[28] His thinking about the affordances of music technology goes back to the 1990s when he had first

---

[28] Windsor and de Bézenac 2012: 108–10.

played around with his sister's Kawai FS610 home keyboard. A memorable function on this keyboard is One Finger Ad-Lib, where pressing a key elicits melodic phrases that suit whatever background rhythm and chords are playing. Also intriguing for Luke was automated arpeggiation. Triggering of arpeggios (sequences of notes derived from chords) was a popular feature of synthesizers in the 1980s, as with one keystroke, players could generate fast and complex repeating patterns. Arpeggios subsequently became a defining ingredient of synthesizer-driven genres such as synthpop, Italo-disco, and techno.

Affordances of this kind have a deeper link to vaporwave's core themes too, as part of a history of labor-saving musical devices. This connection adds further poignance to *BUY NOW*'s acknowledgment of the "anonymous craftsmen" behind capitalism's soundtrack. Synthesizers' and drum machines' democratizing potential has been justly celebrated, but there was another side. The rise of digital technology, Timothy Taylor observes, went hand in hand with economic logic.[29] Soon after their introduction, electronic instruments were recognized as a means of lowering production costs, especially in industries where music needed to be created quickly or in bulk, such as for television, radio, and background music. The new technologies empowered an individual freelancer to replicate what had previously required many musicians. The synthesizer string pad—a patch that creates a chordal wash of sound akin to orchestral strings—is a key example. String players, according to Taylor's informants in the American industry, became the

[29] Taylor 2016: 135–45.

first cohort of studio musicians to lose work in large numbers during the 1980s and others followed.[30] The development of MIDI, music automation, and DAWs was similarly predicated on the efficiencies they might offer. The musical qualities of vaporwave's source inspirations are thus shaped by the logic of capitalism: efficiencies are coded into their very sound.

BUY NOW can therefore be seen as dealing not only with the language of persuasion but also with technological rationalization. The fingerprints can be found across the album. There is extensive use of arpeggiation, and the MIDI generators also leave behind their own digital artifacts signifying labor savings. For instance, while Luke revoices, inverts, or otherwise adjusts the ChordSpace MIDI, in many cases he retains the plain tetrachords. These don't exhibit the variation or inner dynamics one would expect from an actual jazz pianist, but they speak for themselves as shortcuts to "jazziness."

Ironies of this kind continue down to an almost molecular level on *BUY NOW*. From the late 1970s onwards, many synthesizers and drum machines relied on short digital recordings (samples) of notes played by session musicians. The LM-1 and LinnDrum, for instance, feature percussion hits performed by session drummer Art Wood.[31] The Korg M1's sounds are similarly based on samples, although the original musicians' identities are in many cases lost to history, including whoever performed for the famous *Seinfeld* slap bass patch.[32] The labor of these musicians represents the ultimate efficiency:

---

[30] Taylor 2016: 138.
[31] LeRoy 2023: 136.
[32] These bass samples have only been traced back as far as the earlier Korg DSS-1 (Vail 2002).

paid once, they get to perform for digital eternity. Strictly speaking, *BUY NOW* is not sample-free but is instead crowded with the sounds of numerous forgotten performers.

Working mixes for six *BUY NOW* tracks were completed by July 2014. But most were not finalized until midway through 2015, several finished only just before mastering in late May. Overall, the album had a gestation of around sixteen months.

Luke has likened his Eyeliner process to "making a watch or a Fabergé egg,"[33] and on *BUY NOW* this fine attention to detail is applied not only to composition and arrangement. Hundreds of other small enhancements were made using signal-processing effects. Luke used both freeware effects plug-ins and professional suites such as Izotope's Ozone 4 for *BUY NOW*, along with Nuendo's own onboard effects. The overall picture here is again revealing: around forty effects plug-ins were used across the album, but each was generally used for only one or two tracks to impart some special quality. They were another way for Luke to craft the distinct sonic worlds of each track. Most often used were chorus, EQ, reverb, and delay effects. Compressors and maximizers were applied to most tracks, too, both increasing average loudness, while maximizers also enhance tonal frequencies and affect the signal gain. Together with exciters, which add tonal distortion, these finishing touches laid a subtle "crustiness" (as Luke terms it) over the tracks. So, while the Eyeliner sound has been characterized for its MIDI clarity, a certain grit and analog warmth is carefully folded into *BUY NOW* too.

---

[33] Gooding 2018.

As an album without lyrics, there were no titles for *BUY NOW*'s tracks readily to hand. Luke decided on them as the music was being composed and produced, the final titles representing a departure from those of *LARP of Luxury*. Having the generic quality of product categories rather than specific products, they reinforce the more impressionistic approach Luke wanted for *BUY NOW*.

Work on sequencing the order of tracks was also threaded into this work. Certain songs became potential album openers or closers. Others he thought of as thematic "pairs," to be sequenced apart from each other. Late in the process, when it became evident that *BUY NOW* would be released on cassette, a midway juncture had to be established. However, the sequence still needed to provide a satisfying overall flow when the digital version was played.

Looking back to *BUY NOW* in 2020, Luke summed it up as "night time music."[34] This perception relates not only to the nightclub vibes of the album's R&B influence, but also to the way he tested mixes on headphones while riding buses back to Skyranch after working for his father in Lower Hutt, the sun setting behind Wellington's high western hills. (Freelance contracts didn't pay all the bills.) He began to conceive of the album on a deeper level as a nocturnal journey, an odyssey from dusk till dawn. It's another layer of meaning—like others canvassed in this chapter—that adds to one's appreciation of *BUY NOW*.

---

[34] Release notes for Eyeliner, *Drop Shadow* (2020).

4 *BUY NOW*

Having explored the broader stylistic brushstrokes of the album and the technology used to make it, the moment has arrived to cue up *BUY NOW*. It's time to spin the tracks, see how each catches the light, and consider how all the facets fit together.

Luke has already given his side of the story. In 2021, he recorded video screencasts for every track to go into the Turnbull Library's *BUY NOW* production archive. Amounting to over 22,000 words of commentary, in these videos Luke discusses his intentions, influences, and techniques. This chapter takes many cues from these resources, but the aim here is to tap into other musical histories and pick up on different details, to provide new pathways for interpreting and enjoying the album.

Toy Dog 4:05

What is a toy dog? And why does *BUY NOW* start with one?

Toy dogs are very small dogs (or breeds), often kept as expensive fashion accessories. They soared in popularity in the 2000s, celebrity owners including Madonna, Britney Spears, and, most famously, Paris Hilton, scion of the Hilton Hotel empire, who launched her own fashion line for "accessory dog" clothing in 2007. In this milieux, toy dogs are living breathing pinups for conspicuous consumption.

They're also loved companions. "Toy Dog" pays specific tribute to Ralph, a Miniature Pinscher given to Luke's partner Chloe as a graduation present in 2013. BUY NOW was mostly composed with Ralph in the room, and he also stars in BUY NOW's promo video, trotting along beneath rotating digital dollar signs and dog bones, his song playing underneath. At the end, Luke takes his own pop starlet turn, cradling Ralph and fixing the camera with a sultry gaze.[1] There's no distanced irony here. BUY NOW starts by rubbing your face in luxury consumption at its cutest, daring you to be cynical, daring you not to be cynical.

"Toy Dog" was finished early during BUY NOW's production. Working titles were "Bliss" and "Showbiz," but the final choice better conveys the track's mid-tempo strut. The opening offers the initial hook, a riff on M1 Metal Bass vaulting rapidly through four octaves, chasing root notes of the chord changes. Slap bass doubles the offbeats and turnaround licks, kick and snare anchor the pulse. The overall effect is a kind of clanky-jerky shuffle, with pads painting in the background with jazzy chords.

The main melody arrives as a camp surprise. The lead instrument is Doot>Dit, an M1 combi that melds piano with human voice samples, ascending from bass "doots" to treble "dits." Luke also doubles the Doot>Dit MIDI with samples of his own vocal doo-dooing, giving the melody its unique personality. Reference points here are animal toys with

---
[1] Rowell and Ward 2015.

programmed barks, meows, and other sounds. But Luke is also alluding to the kitschy use of human voice samples loaded into keyboards in 80s pop music. Melodies played with "doo-doo" samples are a favorite subcategory of his, examples including "The Voice" by Telex (1988) and "Sensation" (1988) by the Fan Club, a New Zealand pop group Luke latched onto growing up. The strongest influence on "Toy Dog" though is Jean-Michel Jarre's "Zoolookologie" from the LP *Zoolook* (1984), made using vocal samples recorded from people from around the world—and the single's campy music video was also a clear inspiration for the *BUY NOW* promo. Like Jarre's orchestration of a sonic human zoo, Luke seems to also have a sincere purpose with all the doo-dooing, asking: Why do we find these sounds so fun, so funny?

Once the basic arrangement of rhythm, pads, and melody is established, "Toy Dog" goes a long way with relatively little. There are three doo-dooing sections, followed on each occasion by something different. First, a breakdown; second, a bridge with amended changes; and finally, back to the original chords for the outro. What holds interest on repeat listens are the accumulating details. Take the slap bass. Essentially a MIDI cut-and-paste job until the breakdown, the bassline subsequently explores the art of programmed slap, adding short fills and slides, and getting flashy during the bridge. Piano stabs build tension, as do various "doo-doo" false starts, such that the full melody's return around 2:44 comes as a sweet little shock. The surprises continue through the final sections, brass blasting out of nowhere to double a bass lick. The track ends with a final gag: three doo-wop-style subwoofer "doos."

A quirky crossbreed of synthpop and 1980s funk, "Toy Dog" stands yapping at the door to BUY NOW. As an opening statement, it's not too demanding, more the promise of fun ahead.

Sneakers for Men   3:47

"Sneakers for Men" takes BUY NOW into the heart of consumer culture. Luke found the title while browsing product categories on Amazon.com, and given the special place of sneakers in the ongoing alliance between popular music and product advertising, it's an inspired choice.

In 1986, US hip-hop group Run-D.M.C. released "My Adidas," a track praising their favorite footwear, the Adidas Superstar. Sneakers were already part of hip-hop's street identity and the track became a hit, boosting sales of Superstars. Run-D.M.C. and Adidas soon sealed the first endorsement deal between a music act and a sports company, collaborating on cross-marketing ventures in which each gained kudos and wealth.[2] Such deals subsequently became common in hip-hop and increasingly prevalent for other genres. Acquiring street cred by association proved useful for clothing and footwear brands, especially after revelations in the 1990s about their use of third-world sweatshops.[3] From the late 1980s, hip-hop also became in vogue with advertisers more broadly, including for brands such as McDonald's and Coca-Cola.[4]

---

[2] Warnett 2016.
[3] Klein 2001: 363–5.
[4] Taylor 2012: 191.

Aptly then, "Sneakers for Men" begins with a hip-hop-style record scratch—but not actual scratching. Instead, what we hear is a scratching sample taken from a ROM dump of the 1996 Yamaha CS1x keyboard that Luke had found online. Its sample origin becomes obvious once we encounter several identical repeats. The use of this "fake version"[5] (Luke's term) is a "wink," a reminder of digital technology's swift assimilation of musical languages into push-button shortcuts. A split second later, a full drums-bass-keyboard arrangement kicks in, carrying us to another warmly remembered passé corner of 1980s and 1990s music. As Luke puts it, "Sneakers for Men" is "an 'uncool on purpose' new jack swing tribute."

New jack swing (NJS) is an R&B-hip-hop hybrid of the 1987–92 period developed by producers such as Teddy Riley and Jam & Lewis. It fused R&B songcraft with hip-hop production employing drum machines and sequencers, with its associated artists including Keith Sweat, Bobby Brown, and Karyn White.[6] After some crossover success, NJS was eventually eclipsed by the early 1990s rise of gangsta rap, hip-hop soul, and grunge. Its aspirational glamour, often infused with Jazz Age imagery, no longer seemed cutting edge. Yet the genre's obsolescence leaves just the right memory trail for vaporwave to follow.

Luke builds his tribute out of classic NJS parts, including a propulsive shuffle rhythm created with programmed hi-hats. There is also the scratching and the bassline, which busily syncopates arpeggios based on the chord progression. Points of comparison might include the energetic bass of Keith

---

[5] Unless otherwise noted, quotes in this chapter are from Luke's screencasts.
[6] Rivers 2018.

Sweat's "I Want Her" (1987) and the jazzy keyboard pads and bells of New Edition's "If It Isn't Love" (1988).

Once the basic ingredients are established, "Sneakers for Men" becomes a surprisingly rich study in theme and variation. There are three chord progressions used: let's call them A, B, and C. The opening progression (A) is Cm^7-Dm^7-Gm^7-Ab^{maj7}; the second (B) substitutes B^{maj9} for the Dm^7; and the third (C) features chord changes in double-time (Fm^7-Ab^{maj7}-Eb^{maj7}-Dm^7) accompanied by descending triads played on bell patches. The overall structure runs ABCC-ABCC-CC-C. It looks simple on paper. But analyzing the MIDI and stems reveals that the arrangement slips into new alignments at almost every turn. The only exactly repeated combination of drum patterns, bass patches, and keyboards is in the two A sections (sixteen measures out of the track's eighty-eight total). Meanwhile, the bells are layered and patterned in at least six separate ways, setting up question-and-answer passages where the replies come as surprising inevitabilities. Rototoms, hand claps, and electric piano glissandi punctuate the track according to their own cycles, too.

It's sophisticated work. The M1-toting Eyeliner "character" emerges as an overachiever, bringing advanced musical instincts to an ostensible NJS hack job. Even the scratch starts to break down after a while, with the Yamaha sample itself being scratched with digital cut-and-pasting. No simple knock-off, "Sneakers for Men" uses a language of pastiche to create a layered and satisfying new work. In *BUY NOW*'s order of proceedings, we now start to see what Luke is up to. (Note: He currently favors Adidas sneakers.)

Pinot Noir   5:33

"Pinot Noir" is *BUY NOW*'s most streamed track by a wide margin. What accounts for its popularity?

Much of the appeal of "Pinot Noir" likely stems from its gorgeous slow-burning groove. It starts with a minor-key bass ostinato. A kick and snare pattern enters, and a keyboard part traces a wandering arpeggio. A pan flute offers a melody, then lush pads unfurl into an echoing distance. The opening minute and a half creates a sensation of speed and comfort, of new vistas being revealed on a long journey. Luke wrote "Pinot Noir" around the same time as he was learning to drive and first experiencing, presumably, the allure of the accelerator pedal.

The production is tasteful, too. There are no kitsch red flags, the track instead picking up on Tangerine Dream's motorik groove and the MIDI jazz fusion of violinist Jean-Luc Ponty, whose *Individual Choice* (1983) album is one of Luke's favorites. Only the pan flute might raise an eyebrow. But even this cliché (one of those "20 sounds that must die") is doubled with a chime patch and finessed with vibrato. This flute is given its own personality.

The seduction continues as, around 1:30, the bass goes into overdrive. The effect is created by Luke increasing the MIDI velocity on the Multibass patch, triggering a slap percussiveness. Above this newly energized rhythm, the tinkling arpeggio, pan flute, and pad sections repeat. Certain pads (Horizontal, Ladies, WindyForte) slur, creating a woozy moment at 2:17 before composure is regained.

"Pinot Noir" hits a crossroads halfway through. The ostinato gives way to a stuttering bassline that takes up a funky interplay with the drums. Momentum is never lost, but there has been a sea change in the track's overall journey from minor to major key tonality. "Pinot Noir" opens in C minor, the ostinato alternating between C and G roots. Arpeggios and pads then introduce notes that imply more harmonically ambiguous Cm^9 and Gm^{11} chords. That new bassline entering halfway through changes the harmonic context again. Featuring mainly root notes and omitting minor thirds, it recasts the pads, when they reappear, more as $E♭^{maj7}/C$ and F/G, with only the pan flute part retaining hints of minor tonality. Anticipation grows and, for the outro, the track modulates decisively into C minor's relative major key of E♭. It's a smoothly handled harmonic ride.

What does any of this have to do with wine? Luke professes fascination with "the idea of wine," which had already inspired "Sauvignon Blanc" from the previous Eyeliner album *LARP of Luxury*. These track titles happen to refer to the two leading grape varieties grown for New Zealand's NZ$2 billion annual-export wine industry. Both are also popular locally and heavily advertised. Pinot noir is an obvious—and subtly local—wine to reference.

Calling a wine "Pinot noir" has a larger context, too. Such varietal labeling was introduced in the 1960s as part of the globalization of wine production, becoming a successful way of marketing wines from New World countries such as the United States, Australia, and New Zealand that could not claim the sort of geographical pedigree applied to wines from traditional European winegrowing areas.[7] Varietal labeling was paralleled by the rise of wine tourism, including vineyard

---

[7] Robinson 2015: 774.

trails, wine festivals, and wine cruise-liner tours. New Zealand has itself become a popular destination on the international circuit.

This is the "idea of wine" that "Pinot Noir" explores: one synonymous with international travel, leisure, and affluence. Ironically, the track cultivates such associations in very generic ways. We could—perhaps more plausibly—be listening to the soundtrack for a high-end car advertisement. The underlying incongruity, how advertising sometimes uses music with little traditional association with the product, may be Luke's point. There is only one explicit sonic reference to wine throughout "Pinot Noir," a reverberant drip sound at 4:05.

From here on, Luke steers "Pinot Noir" further into marketing fantasyland. A celestial choir beams down, while steel drums play reggae offbeats. Crickets emerge from the background. Are we perhaps on a wine cruise in the Caribbean (hardly noted for its wineries)? "Pinot Noir" thus reaches its ironic climax. Yet how easy it has been to succumb to this intoxicating ride and those tropical finishing notes.

High Heels   2:40

As Luke was producing *BUY NOW*, he identified certain tracks as "pairs." In the album's final sequence, these were spaced apart to avoid repetition and create subtle payoffs for attentive listeners. "Sneakers for Men" and "High Heels" are the first obvious examples. Paired thus, their shared theme emerges as the gendering of footwear. The title of "Sneakers for Men" is a dig at the marketing assumption that sneakers are male footwear by default, while "High Heels" turns to the female market. "It's about this really strange view of 'femininity' that I grew up with in advertising," Luke comments. "Where all women need to be easy-breezy . . . this sort of 'professional woman.' But it was all sort of naïve and kinda gross."

Such TV advertisements are part of a longer trend—beginning with the 1970s advocacy of US marketeer Rena Bartos—to diversify representations of women, mostly portrayed until then in domestic or marital roles, a key aim being to reach the lucrative new working-woman market.[8] A common approach, as Luke alludes to, was to glamorize the multiple roles a contemporary woman might have to take, with peppy, soulful music often being employed. Growing up, Luke probably encountered local examples such as the 1993 TV commercial for Columbine hosiery, with its Latin-tinged "Do the Columbine" song.[9] Stylistically even closer to "High Heels" is a 1990 Salon Selectives advert of US origin whose jazz-pop theme was sung by artist Phoebe Snow. "Today, some women will leave for work looking like they've just stepped out of a salon," the narrator declares.

In reimagining this aesthetic, "High Heels" takes its cues from the dance-pop end of 1980s R&B. After the opening electric piano simmers and the slap bass restlessly twitches, the track kicks into a wonderfully sassy keyboard-brass riff. A comparison might be the slow-countdown-to-brass-liftoff of Whitney Houston's "I Wanna Dance with Somebody" (1987). "High Heels" is also strewn with the kind of attention-grabbing

---

[8] Leppert 2019: 10–3.
[9] Sung by local pop-star Fiona McDonald (Headless Chickens, Straw People).

techniques—brass stabs, harp glissandi, bass pops, tom hits—that Luke gained familiarity with for his freelance contracts. A heavily slurred brass stab around 1:10 is an outré touch, one that might support a sexual innuendo in one of those 1990s adverts. Throughout, the drums have the punchiness of the classic 1980s gated-reverb effect (another "sound that must die"). "Nice and hype-y," Luke confirms. "Make it sound like advertising."

Yet despite the brazen sales pitch, it's hard to resist "High Heels." There is a catchy main melody and funky arrangement, plus delicate cadences in the passing chords. Luke's duty of musical care is most evident in the track's highlight, a chromatic harmonica solo, played with the M1 OnTheRoad patch, inspired by Stevie Wonder's solo in the Eurythmics hit "There Must Be an Angel (Playing with My Heart)" (1985). Slowing the pace to half-time, Luke guides the eighteen-second solo through opening swoops into a series of pedal-point figures. The MIDI programming is impressive: around 200 tiny adjustments were made to replicate the harmonica's sour-sweet quality.

Luke found "High Heels" irresistible, too. One early mix for the track increases the tempo, another slows it down with chopping-and-screwing. He went with neither: "It sounds too good in the proper tempo." Then, as if to conform with the duration of a TV ad, the track, with a categorical bass flourish, stops.

Payphone 6:20

Listening to telephone hold music is a near-universal experience. People may cumulatively spend days (perhaps months) of their lives regaled with stock music, playlists, or radio feeds, waiting to be connected. "Payphone," *BUY NOW*'s longest track, is a study in these musical limbos.

Hold music can be vexing, but as the original inventor Alfred Levy realized, waiting in silence was worse, creating uncertainty and losing business when people hung up in exasperation. Music was the obvious way "to pacify... and also to while away the idle time of the caller," Levy noted in his 1966 patent.[10] Systems playing hold-music loops were introduced in the 1980s, the most renowned example entering service a few years later. In 1989, inspired by Greek new-age artist Yanni, California high-school student Tim Carleton composed "Opus No.1" on his Yamaha DX7.[11] It was recorded by a friend, Darrick Deel, who went on to work for the digital telco Cisco. When Cisco's IP phone service was introduced in 1998, Deel arranged for "Opus No.1" to become the default hold music. Carleton's track now features on over 100 million phone sets worldwide. It is one of the most pervasive musical recordings of our time.

"Opus No.1" has also attracted a cult following among vaporwave artists, with a faithful cover version by Eyeliner featuring on the 2020 compilation *Thank You for Holding* released by UK label My Pet Flamingo. "Payphone" also takes inspiration from "Opus No.1," with its slow tempo, placid groove, and echoing handclaps. But the track also displays a deeper understanding of what has made "Opus" so successful.

An atmosphere of gentle melancholy is a crucial feature, both tracks featuring subdued minor-key harmony. "Payphone"

---

[10] Levy 1966.
[11] Corbett 2014.

centers around B♭m⁹ and Fm⁹ chords, with the wistful main melody lent substance by the Jazz Grand Piano A patch from Steinberg's HALionOne VST. It sets a mood that might reassure callers that their time is being taken seriously: that even in the hold queue you get Grade-A service. Compositional structure is crucial, too. Hold music typically uses repeating loops but, as many people will attest to, overly short loops soon become annoying. Like "Opus," "Payphone" takes a more sophisticated approach. It features enough repetition to "pacify" that hypothetical caller, but also enough variation to keep them interested and hanging on the line.

The seed of the track was MIDI automatically generated by Band-in-a-Box. Initially, Luke looped a forty-second section with heavy hypnagogic-style reverb. Such a rudimentary approach, he soon realized, wasn't very compelling, and the final version instead carefully spins out the core material. The build is gradual. String pads play lush voicings, bass and drums take their own good time to join, with snare-drum sidestick suggesting a ticking clock. Only at 0:52 does the main piano melody appear. After a shorter second section, the track cycles through again, new touches laid in as we go, leading to other bridges and repeats. Additional instruments double the now-familiar melody. Short glissandi ornament the theme too, played by the Stero Harp, Stero Vibe, and DigitalBox patches. "Payphone" thus slowly transforms as it majestically rolls onwards.

The track's melancholy also derives from the nostalgia implicit in its title. Payphones were a once common public facility now largely supplanted by cell phones. They are emblematic too, Luke observes, of other "small public technological spaces" that offer refuge from the surrounding world, such as elevators, and the glissandi in "Payphone" were partly intended to suggest elevator chimes. Such connections raise the postironic possibility that hold music, rather than being a time-wasting aural sedative, is also a kind of haven, an opportunity for contemplation. "Payphone" hints at this idea by incorporating elements from new-age music: the pads and reverb-drenched piano, and the pentatonic glissandi, reminiscent of a Japanese koto. Recordings of thunder and rain are also layered beneath sections from 3:50 onwards. These are a classic new-age ingredient, with the rainstorm becoming a natural metaphor for the tumultuous world that "Payphone" offers refuge from.

The track closes with a lengthy outro of chords and a rainstorm. For those listening to *BUY NOW* on cassette or vinyl, "Payphone" also ends Side A. The album thus includes its own "hold" experience, during which you can physically turn over the album, the luxurious sounds of "Payphone" fading in your ears.

Venetian Blinds   3:58

We begin Side B in a different musical limbo, one of suspense. An organ pad and bass cast background shadows. Trap hi-hats fidget. A marimba starts up a nagging motif.

"Venetian Blinds," as the title suggests, is a homage to film noir, specifically American "Eighties Noir."[12] A successor to the

---

[12] Arnett 2020: 67–84.

Hollywood noirs of the 1940s and 1950s, Eighties Noir explored "the dark side of Reagan's America": the dangers lurking within a media-saturated society obsessed with consumerism.[13] An eye for the dazzling yet deceptive surfaces of modern life was a signature feature, and synthesizer soundtracks were another. The work of filmmaker Michael Mann is a case in point, including *Thief* (1981, score by Tangerine Dream) and *Manhunter* (1986, score by Michel Rubini), and the TV series *Miami Vice* (1984–9), featuring Czech-born Jan Hammer's theme and cues. *Vice* itself took much inspiration from Brian De Palma's version of *Scarface* (1983), scored by Italian disco producer Giorgio Moroder. These soundtracks are now touchstones for vaporwave and synthwave, along with the South Florida iconography of palm-tree sunsets, pastels, and neon.

So, what Eighties Noir scenario did Luke have in mind for "Venetian Blinds"? In his commentary, he mentions a detective stakeout of a kidnapping or drug deal: "someone peering through venetian blinds." He also cites voyeuristic scenes from De Palma's thriller *Body Double* (1984, score by Pino Donaggio). The Eyeliner brief? To supply "cheap synthesizer music." Of course, as with previous tracks, the final product becomes something of a creative overachievement.

"Venetian Blinds" begins by honoring suspense conventions. The opening pad shifts back and forth between chords of ease (Ab^6) and solemnity (Cm), like a cop checking a potential crime scene through the blinds: waiting, checking, waiting. A marimba motif in parallel thirds raises tension, altering the

---

[13] Arnett 2020: 68.

tonic chord to A♭⁶ᐟ⁹ every second eighth-note. The atmosphere of ticking suspense is not unlike that conveyed by a Jan Hammer *Miami Vice* cue such as "Clues." Then a chord change and a slap bass riff: heart rates quicken. The brass patch All-n-One! intrudes, garishly bending in pitch. Then it's back to more waiting, checking. The UnisonSawLD patch screams out a lick, over and over, and what sounds like heavy footsteps intrude. More pitch-bent brass follows, then UnisonSawLD doubles the bassline like a neon highlighter. A violent climax seems imminent.

Up until now, how has "cheapness" been conveyed? Through those "super hammy" (Luke's term) brass pitch-bends, for one. Synthesizer slurring, bending, and sliding was something of an Eighties Noir cliché for suggesting sleaze or foreboding, or to emphasize a disturbing revelation. Examples include "Night Ride (Reprise)" from *American Gigolo* (1980, score by Moroder) and the dread-inducing bends of the *Unsolved Mysteries* TV series theme (by Michael Boyd and Gary Remal Malkin). The UnisonSawLD lick is a more obscure riff on "cheapness." It actually derives from the Korg demo melody "40 Sequence)(" that Luke accidentally triggered in the Nuendo DAW at one point. Creative pride might normally preclude the borrowing of a stock demo, but here "40 Sequence)(" fits the bargain-basement brief and the track's lurid atmosphere. True to form though, Luke devises a more sophisticated arrangement, hocketing the lick's MIDI between three patches to give it a twinkling, metropolitan quality.

Returning to that imminent climax, "Venetian Blinds" suddenly launches into rapid-fire trance keyboards. A rave has broken out. Then it's back to more waiting, checking. The hocketed lick returns, but more subdued. The stakeout winds down, the cops go home.

The "empty climax" of "Venetian Blinds," as Luke calls it, makes its own ironic comment. The track can be interpreted as a satire on how Eighties Noir soundtracks were made to carry so much existential dread and doomed worldview. Significantly, an early mix included a pounding snare beat, reminiscent of somber *Miami Vice* anthems like "Evan" or "Graham's Theme" from *Manhunter*. But Luke removed the beat—and with it the dread. We still get to savor those other adrenaline-inducing musical gestures but, in the end, nobody gets hurt. Even so, we are left wondering what *BUY NOW* has next in store. "Venetian Blinds" foreshadows the thematic complexity and darker orchestrations of *BUY NOW*'s second half. This show ain't over yet.

Showbiz   4:21

Luke clearly wanted to hang onto the title "Showbiz," recycling it from "Toy Dog" and as a potential album title. One can see why: "Showbiz" is loaded with meaning. The idea that the "show" cannot be separated from the "business" obviously resonates with *BUY NOW*'s vaporwave themes.

"Showbiz" was itself originally named "Tap Dancin'," both titles relating to an earlier musical talking point among Luke's circle. "Top hat" is a retrospective genre label that Luke gives to 1980s–1990s pop music that references the jazz-cabaret music of the Roaring Twenties-Great Depression era. Examples include Taco's "Puttin' on the Ritz" (1983), Kid Creole and the

Coconuts, tuxedo-clad Italo-disco artists like Gazebo, and Madonna's music video for "Hanky Panky" (1990), with new jack swing hits like Bobby Brown's "My Prerogative" (1988) being close cousins. These dalliances with the Jazz Age are the starting point for Eyeliner's study in dance-floor hedonism, "Showbiz."

Top hat and cane in hand, the track kicks off with a descending pizzicato bassline on Super Bass, the MIDI swing setting dialed up. The shuffle feel is then fortified with a four-on-the-floor disco beat. Vibraphones add a subtle 1930s evocation, marking out a pattern of three-against-four displaced accents akin to the melody of "In the Mood," made famous by bandleader Glenn Miller. In the second section of "Showbiz" (beginning 0:30), bass and vibes combine for a robotic-sounding riff in C minor. Tap has given way to rave, to "shuffle" in the sense of German *schaffel* techno or EDM dance steps like the Melbourne Shuffle. On cue, a synth patch (UniPizz JS-Y) with a low-pass filter takes over from vibes and then delivers the track's lead melody. This synth melody pays tribute to instrumental electro classics such as Harold Faltermeyer's "Axel F" (1984), but the melodic structure also suggests an older question-and-answer tradition. Prompted by hand claps, the melody repeats a "question" three times and a concluding lick "answers" and is then "answered" again with sampled "hey" vocals on the offbeats. The entire Q&A structure then moves up and down octaves, recreating the "Q&A" on a larger scale. While the synths are modern, we aren't too far removed here from swing-era showbiz. Luke mentions that the riff reminds him of old jazz standards, and it carries something of the bluesy call-and-response of, say, "Minnie the Moocher."

A third of the way through and we've already covered a lot of ground. It's time to revisit the premise. What lay behind the tacky microgenre that Luke and his friends identified? Why were those 1980s musicians looking back to the 1920s–1930s period? The periods have much in common, the 1920s–1930s and the 1980s both being eras of boom-bust economics, high extravagance and deep inequality, hyper-optimism, and glamorous criminality. Each also produced razzle-dazzle pop culture. They were times when escapism was the business of show business, and whether in the clubs of the Jazz Age or the Decade of Greed, the euphoria of dance was an important medium of escape. By tracing a thread through swing jazz, disco, electro, and EDM, Luke draws out this dance history further. As Luke knew well from his hundreds of Disasteradio shows, dance still sells. After the 2008 Global Financial Crisis, the business case was the same, and "Showbiz" is where *BUY NOW* gets down to business with its most dancefloor-ready track.

The remainder of "Showbiz" pulls the thread tighter. The "In the Mood" triads take an extended reprise, and UniPizz returns with more filter-sweeping attitude. At 2:13, there's a drop. It lasts all of one second, Luke's "wink" at EDM conventions. The groove hardens up with a slap-inflected bass (KillerBass). More filter-sweeping on the UniPizz riff which then—in classic techno fashion—starts octave-hopping itself. Then the breakdown.

"Showbiz" has doffed its hat to various dance styles throughout the track. The finale is where singularity is achieved. Post-breakdown, everything returns for one big production number. The triumphant finale is reinforced in the low end by FilmScore, another much-used and abused M1 combi. The final chords ring out, and the cast holds the pose. Curtain. That's showbiz.

Windchimes   3:21

Until now, the predominant influences on *BUY NOW* have been American R&B and European synthesizer music. "Windchimes" carries us to another area of cultural interest for Luke: Japan, the Land of Korg.

Japanese computer games, Walkmans, electronic keyboards, and the blockbuster anime *Akira* (1988) all cropped up in Luke's early life, with Japan's burgeoning cultural influence on the West during the 1980s and 1990s coinciding with the millennial generation's formative years. Other vaporwave artists have drawn heavily from Japanese culture for their artwork, album titles, and especially the use of scripts such as kanji. This influence has been characterized as a kind of "techno-orientalism," injecting a dystopian sense of "eastern technological advancement" into the vaporwave imaginary.[14] Luke has rarely dabbled in these motifs, however. Instead, it's Japanese music that has had more impact, especially examples that unsettle notions of Japanese cultural authenticity.

"Windchimes" is principally a homage to family-friendly anime soundtracks. In his commentary, Luke cites Hayao Miyazaki's celebrated film *My Neighbor Totoro* (1988), with its score by frequent Miyazaki collaborator Joe Hisaishi, as

---

[14] Kim 2020.

the archetypal case. Mainly employing Western orchestral and popular idioms, Hisaishi's soundtracks also feature what Kunio Hara calls his "minimal and ethnic" style. These cues might sound "Japanese" to Western ears but are inspired by US minimalist composers like Terry Riley and Steve Reich, who were themselves influenced by Indonesian gamelan and other Southeast Asian music.[15] Named after a globally popular instrument with vaguely Asian new-age associations, "Windchimes" is an apt title for exploring this multicultural hall of mirrors, to which Luke adds his own vaporwave reflections.

"Windchimes" has one of *BUY NOW*'s simplest structures. To start, the M1 Candle pad and HALionOne Synth Bass spell out chord changes. Then the main melody plays twice. This structure gets repeated (with Slap'n'Thump added), a bridge following with new changes, countermelody, and solo—and then we're back to the main theme and fade. With its short melodies, "Windchimes" comes across like a super-truncated facsimile of songs such as *Totoro*'s "Path of the Wind" or the title tune from *Laputa: Castle in the Sky* (1986, score also by Hisaishi).

The abbreviated quality very much suits the Eyeliner brief. Rather than a full-blown anime anthem, Eyeliner has been tasked with creating something humbler: Luke's commentary refers to an accompaniment for a credits sequence or "a montage where nothing [in] particular happens"—the cinematic equivalent of hold music. "Windchimes" and "Payphone," in fact, form a pair on *BUY NOW*. As laid-back interstitial music, both are sequenced to provide respite from busier tracks on either side.

---

[15] Hara 2020: 30.

How does "Windchimes" evoke Japanese anime music? Most obviously by emulating the instrumentation and rhythms of Hisaishi's "minimal and ethnic" style, which weaves together percussion reminiscent of gamelan, tabla, and other non-Western examples into tapestries of overlapping sequencer patterns.[16] Luke employs similar patches. The "Windchimes" melody is played with Moon-Night (combi of Gamelan, Music Box, and Slap Bass); the countermelody with Caribbean (steel drums); and chord offbeats with East&West (combi of FingCymbal and HamDulcimer). Woodblock and tambourine add another "ethnic" layer above the kick and snare. And, keeping things efficient, the same drum-fill repeats throughout. Like "Payphone," "Windchimes" was seeded from Band-in-a-Box MIDI: cut-and-pasting the fill here signifies a speedy, economical process.

Also subtly evoking "Japanese music" is the bridge's combination of melody and harmony. One technique Luke particularly admires of Japanese game-music composers such as Nobuo Uematsu (*Final Fantasy*) is using chord changes to wring the most out of simple melodies. "Windchimes" offers a demonstration in miniature with its nineteen-second solo on the Crazy SOLO patch. The solo consists of fourteen notes with only five pitches between them. However, played over the bridge changes (E^9sus^4-Bm^7-A^{maj9}-$C^{\sharp}m^7$), these five pitches end up occupying eleven different scale degrees, thus leaving an impression of greater melodic variety. Like much else with "Windchimes," the solo makes a little go a long way.

---

[16] Hara 2020: 30–1, 70–1.

Chit Chat 3:47

With "Chit Chat," we return to advertising, though not, it should be noted, for the Chit Chat chocolate biscuits made by New Zealand company Griffin's. "Chit Chat" is not really about any specific product. It's best considered a fantasia inspired by advertising music's avant-garde tendencies.

As discussed in Chapter 3, music in TV advertising changed in the 1980s and 1990s. One trend was brands seeking to convey a sense of hip irony to appeal to younger audiences jaded by hard-sell consumerism, with artists known for their dissident music being courted by advertisers. Some refused to "sell out," as when the Wieden+Kennedy agency attempted to woo Negativland to advertise Miller beer.[17] However, others saw such offers as consistent with their artistic aims of subverting mainstream culture from the inside. One artist riding this trend was Mark Mothersbaugh, founding member of one of Luke's favorite bands, Devo.

When Devo went into a hiatus around 1986, Mothersbaugh found success with TV advertising work and established his own production house, Mutato Muzika. He went on to score hundreds of adverts and numerous movies and TV shows, bringing humor, experimentalism, and pop-culture expertise to the task.[18] (Such crossovers are another reason why advertising and popular music now appear so intertwined.) Luke admires this side of Mothersbaugh's music too, with his own advertising work also tending toward quirky

---
[17] Klein 2001: 330–1.
[18] Dellinger and Giffels 2003: 204–5.

pastiches. "Chit Chat" picks up where "Toy Dog" left off by paying further tribute to voice-sample composition, such as features prominently in Mothersbaugh's work, from his first advertisement (for Hawaiian Punch in 1987) through to the theme tune for the 1990s *Rugrats* TV series, and beyond.

"Chit Chat" originated with an unreleased composition, "Energy Star," which itself derives from an earlier Nuendo sketch. Over repeated chord changes common to all three (A^6-A-F$^\sharp$m-G^6-G), Luke convenes "Chit Chat"'s quirky sonic soirée. The overall trajectory for the first two-thirds of the track is toward increasing complexity. We start with arpeggios (on Pizzo Hut and Soloist); then the bass plays chord roots with a Scotch snap-type rhythm; and then drums enter. The rhythmic feel is unusual. The drums play half-time beneath sixteenth-note arpeggios, the track seeming to operate at different tempos simultaneously. Luke borrowed the technique from tracks such as "Light in Darkness" (1982) by Japanese synthpop group Yellow Magic Orchestra, the result being slightly uncomfortable, like a composed equivalent for the chopped-and-screwed effect. The social ice—as it were—has not yet been broken.

The chit-chat starts up around 1:13. First, the bassline breaks into a four-octave conversation with itself. Kick drum doubles the bass' rhythm, dialoguing with the steady snare beat. Trebling the bass rhythm is the M1's default voice-sample patch, Voice Wave, with a four-octave melody that manifests as several distinct "voices" conversing. The arrangement showcases Luke's practice of copying and pasting sections of MIDI, assigning different patches to the copies, and then muting and adjusting notes for each. At 1:50, *Rugrats*-style chatter enters. Luke has cloned the MIDI yet again, assigning samples of his own voice ("ahh," "baa," "bee," "bo") to join the confab, one by one. The result is like a chorus of frogs, chipmunks, and other creatures. Then, without warning, the snare-drum tempo doubles to common time. "Like . . . a piece of ad music where the resolution happens," Luke comments, "the call gets answered"—by the advertised product, of course.

"Chit Chat" also brings elements from across BUY NOW into dialogue. So far, we have voice samples from "Toy Dog," a stuttering bass somewhat like that in the second half of "Pinot Noir," plus the arpeggios and offbeat chords found throughout the album. Next, the "top hat" groove of "Showbiz" arrives with a pizzicato riff played on pan flute and yet more voice samples. The track is a veritable hubbub by now. Some decorum is needed. It arrives in the form of a chorus of sopranos, who transport "Chit Chat" decorously through to its conclusion.

Those voice samples cannot be held down, though. They return to trade banter in the final measures, finishing with barking. All that late-night partying seems to have woken up the neighbor's dog (perhaps a toy dog?). The last word goes to Slap'n'Thump though, which has been absent until now. For "Chit Chat" to be on BUY NOW, slap bass needs to front up, so Luke adds a couple of hits as a final wink.

Private Hospital   1:16

Luke describes "Private Hospital" as "a quick little tune." The shortest and simplest track on BUY NOW, it helps put some space between neighboring cuts, both complex. Yet "Private

Hospital" is far from filler. There is something ominous about arriving at a hospital so late in the piece. In terms of the album's nocturnal journey, it's just before dawn.

"Private Hospital" was conceived to be the theme music for an imagined 1980s–1990s TV medical drama. Luke had explored a similar idea before with Disasteradio's "Marathon," the ostensible theme for a made-up series about a crime-solving athlete with a bionic leg. For BUY NOW, a hospital-drama appealed, contrasting with the crime noir of "Venetian Blinds," the album's other TV-show track (and "Private Hospital"'s pair). Healthcare was also in Luke's background: both his mother and sister worked at Hutt Hospital. Lastly, the subject was topical, as he'd recently had a protracted struggle with the state insurer ACC (Accident Compensation Corporation) over coverage for knee surgery.

Setting a hospital series at a private institution is a significant choice in the context of vaporwave's capitalist critique. Most medical dramas are set at public or charity-based hospitals, with one notable exception being New Zealand's longest-running soap opera, *Shortland Street* (theme music by Graham Bollard). When it began in 1992, *Shortland Street* was based at a private clinic of the kind then being established under neoliberal governments seeking to make healthcare more "user pays."[19]

"Private Hospital" is based around a riff on the E.pianoMix patch. Simple changes (Cm^7-Ab^{maj7}-$Bbsus^4$) repeat throughout. The arrangement has affinities with James Newton Howard's piano-led theme for US medical drama *ER* (1994–2009), also

---

[19] Dunleavy 2005: 235–7.

harking back to 1980s smooth-jazz themes like for *Hill Street Blues* (1981–7, theme by Mike Post). The production values are set more at the soap-opera level though. Although the arrangement features some variety, including an urgent middle section where the piano drops away and Slap'n'Thump plays octaves for a syncopated echo effect, a thinly veiled tawdriness prevails. A recurring melodramatic drum-fill registers initially as a sample akin to Mike Post's subway-train sounds in the *NYPD Blue* theme, but the effect is more a cheap recreation created with widely panned rapid tom-drum hits. Approaching the climax, Luke pulls out the stops with a portentous FilmScore part, support from pan flute and vibrato brass, and more stereo toms unleashed as a parting flourish.

In 2000, *Shortland Street*'s private clinic changed to a public hospital, paralleling a real-world shift away from neoliberal healthcare policies in New Zealand. "Private Hospital" looks back to an earlier time when it seemed that free-market approaches might rejuvenate New Zealand's health system, even lend it a degree of soap-opera glamour. In the post-GFC 2010s, such ideas are harder to sell, with the glamour long tarnished. Nonetheless, Eyeliner does their best for "Private Hospital" on the limited budget allocated.

Pictionary 4:30

"Pictionary" looks back—and looks forward. As with "Chit Chat," it draws together threads from earlier tracks but weaves these into a new pattern: a vaporwave study in ambient and new age to round out the album.

The title "Pictionary" comes from the best-selling US board game first released in 1985. *Pictionary* involves teams competing by having to guess words based on quick drawings before sand drains away through an hourglass. "Pictionary" the Eyeliner track is about images too according to Luke, more specifically those with indeterminate meanings: "enigmas . . . mirages . . . optical illusions."

The track begins softly. First, the Mallet Magic combi fades in: vibraphone and kalimba playing an ostinato, with a pad in the background. The Willow combi joins, tweaked to suggest a pan flute sliding between pitches in a way reminiscent of a shakuhachi. The ostinato has a non-Western tilt too. Luke had been listening to Steve Reich's *Six Marimbas* (1986), a work influenced by Balinese gamelan,[20] and jazz fusion guitarist Steve Tibbetts's kalimba-laden "Any Minute" (1984), and "Pictionary" has a similar feeling of gentle harmonic suspensions: Mallet Magic plays a D minor triad first inversion, Willow extending this into the less resolved territories of Dm^7 and Dm^{add11}. The overall effect is reminiscent of certain tracks from Aphex Twin's *Selected Ambient Works Volume II* (1994).

Something awakens at 0:50. MultiBass strikes up an ominous bassline with a touch of slap, Pianology bringing an insistent melody. Other instruments step out of the shadows, thick synth tones from Willow and Stero Vibe assuming the ostinato. One might say the hourglass has been turned and the game has begun. The change ushers in another influence: the soundtrack for the CD-ROM adventure game *Myst* (1993). Composed by the game's developer Robyn Miller, its

---

[20]Tenzer 2019.

minor-key inexorability famously enhances the spookiness of *Myst*'s deserted landscapes.

Myst and *Pictionary* are both games about clarifying what we are looking at. Luke similarly sets up musical illusions for us to ponder in "Pictionary." Is Willow's flute rising and falling, or falling and rising? Both, it turns out: there are two flutes moving in contrary motion. "Pictionary"'s melody is another puzzle. It picks out notes above an A natural pedal, posing an ostensible "question" and then "answering" with a twice-repeated phrase, but then the melodic structure starts to mutate. Notes from the melody are flipped above and below the pedal, tracking in parallel, contrary motion, and combinations of both. Like teams trying to guess words in *Pictionary*, the melody has become a series of evolving problems and conjectures. In these and other ways, "Pictionary" increases in complexity over a relatively static harmonic base.

Musical genre is a final enigma: how genre labels alter our perspective on music that might sound very similar. Initially, the track's most obvious genre connections are with ambient music and adventure-game soundtracks. But the sound of a river also runs through it. Heard from the middle section on, this natural sound effect is more associated with new-age music. Hugely popular in the 1980s–1990s, hugely derided as spiritual fluff, new-age has recently been recuperated by vaporwave artists (among others) for its synthesizer language and kitsch reputation. As Luke asks in his commentary: "why not write music with respect to nature? 'The awesome force of nature.'" Applying a different genre label has again altered perceptions of "Pictionary." And as the outro trails off, some final sounds emerge. Modulating the length of a double-delay effect on a pan flute, Luke summons up what sounds like a dawn chorus of birds above the river. New Zealand listeners will recognize the native tui's call.

"Pictionary" thus leaves us with some final thoughts as the sun lightens the sky. In using synthesizers to foster environmental consciousness, whether for the ambient chillout, to provoke awe in a game world, or for new-age edification, isn't it all some kind of spiritual quest? Isn't it all about chasing some ghost through the machine? As dawn breaks on *BUY NOW*, such questions are left hanging in the air for another day.

5 Showbiz

May 2015: Eyeliner's *BUY NOW* was ready for the world. It was showbiz time. How the album was released and what followed—the reviews, ratings, streams, reissues, remixes, and uploads—rounds out its story.

Such matters bring the twenty-first-century music economy into view. The Internet has been a hugely disruptive force over the last twenty-five years. Early on, applications such as Napster, which enabled the free sharing of personal MP3 libraries, were blamed for threatening the recording industry's very existence. Yet new paradigms have also emerged: streaming has become the primary way people now access music recordings, and self-release platforms have thrived, as have labels specializing in vintage physical formats such as vinyl and cassette. The infrastructure of critical reception has evolved too, the web both undermining traditional journalism and offering new forms of evaluation and commentary.

These are among the contexts this chapter explores in relation to *BUY NOW*. Given the album's title, it's also only appropriate to "follow the money" and look at how Luke is paid for his artistic labor. More than financial reward is involved here, though. *BUY NOW* exemplifies the multifarious paybacks for musical creativity in the digital age.

The story of *BUY NOW*'s release begins with some label dealings. Eyeliner's first two albums had been released on Crystal Magic

Records, and *BUY NOW* might have been the third. During the album's gestation, Luke sent mixes to CMR's Fraser Austin and recalls playing him the near-finished album at a Skyranch social gathering in April 2015. But Luke felt there was less than 100 percent enthusiasm. The reason was potentially unrelated to perceptions of musical quality as, behind the scenes, CMR was starting to demand more attention than Austin could commit to any longer (and, as it happened, six months later he closed the label down).[1]

Luke next approached Beer on the Rug. Based in Lawrence (Kansas), they were an experimental music label not unlike CMR, operating on a small scale outside the industry, doing limited-edition physical releases, and using Bandcamp as a shopfront. Founded in 2011 by musicians Gaurav Bashyakarla and Josh Thomas, Beer on the Rug (BOTR) had released the early vaporwave of Computer Dreams, Boy Snacks, and others who had served as Luke's introduction to the genre. The genre-defining album *Floral Shoppe* was another BOTR classic.

Three years later, as part of his reconsideration of vaporwave for *BUY NOW*, Luke had returned to these albums. "It made a lot of sense if I was responding to all that stuff," he told Zac Arnold in 2015, "to be included as part of the label."[2] He wasn't cold calling either. Back in 2013, after *High Fashion Mood Music* came out, Bashyakarla had made contact to see if Luke wanted to do a release. Two years later, there was still interest.

Luke also finalized the album's title. "Pictionary" had been one working title, "Showbiz" another. Fresh inspiration again

---

[1] Fraser Austin, pers. comm. September 22, 2023.
[2] Arnold 2015.

came from the retail website Amazon. Browsing one day with the express-purchase option turned on, Luke started thinking about the button on every product page with the text "Buy Now." The perfect digital-age *détournement* beckoned: "If I called the album 'BUY NOW,'" he realized, "there would always be these little billboards for the record embedded in all these websites." It was as plain a statement as you could get of neoliberal capitalism's pressure to consume, especially when spelled out, like many other vaporwave titles and artist names, in "attention-craving capital letters."[3]

Beer on the Rug released *BUY NOW* as a digital download on their Bandcamp page on June 27, 2015 (catalog number BOTR036), with a limited-edition cassette following on July 7. The album arrived with striking artwork: no other vaporwave album looks quite like *BUY NOW*. An homage to 1980s design, the cover was created by the New York-based studio EyeBodega. Scanning BOTR's recent catalog, Luke had been especially impressed by their work for Euglossine's *Complex Playground* (2015). After a rather monochromatic initial mockup, EyeBodega broke out the primary hues and pastels with a design that evokes postmodern stylists like the Memphis Group (an influential Italian design group active 1980–7). Swatch watches are another influence, the cover's eyes mimicking the faces of two Swatches: Needles and Flumotions (both 1988). The teal background was inspired by another Swatch but is also reminiscent of Tiffany Blue. Long associated with fabled New York jeweler Tiffany & Co., this shade of eggshell blue has been a protected trademark since

---

[3] Harper 2012a.

1998. *BUY NOW*'s cover thus neatly ties together the 1980s period, a sense of playful facsimile, and luxury branding.

BUY NOW's release went well, but behind the scenes, issues arose. Racking up several hundred units sold in those first months, the proceeds were apparently not flowing back to Luke and he eventually canceled BOTR's control over digital sales.[4] Given the Internet's scope for self-distribution, this episode raises the question: What was the appeal of being on a label in the first place?

Over the course of his career, Luke has pursued a largely independent path. In the early Disasteradio days, he had distributed tracks as free downloads using various now-defunct websites, initially MP3.com, followed by MP3.com.au, BeSonic.com, and others. Following DIY-punk precedent, he also burned CD–Rs to sell at gigs and through Red Letter Distro.

Collaboration with labels had started with the 2005 Disasteradio compilation *Datasette*, released by New Zealand indie Stink Magnetic. Ian Jorgenson's A Low Hum put out several later albums. These labels had provided moral support and, for physical releases, fronted manufacturing costs, done promotion, and organized distribution. Traditional record-label deals were not involved, though. Not needing an advance to cover recording costs, Luke retained all rights over the music, with any profits from sales being shared. He also undertook his own online distribution through a Bandcamp Disasteradio

---

[4] Attempts were made to contact Beer on the Rug, without success.

page (established 2009), using an aggregation service to place music with streaming platforms.

Labels have served similar functions for Eyeliner, but additional factors are also in play. Vaporwave has always been a prolific genre. The Internet Archive's Vapor Vault collection contains 3,399 recordings for the period between 2011 and 2015, the year of *BUY NOW*'s release. The cumulative total almost doubles by the following year. In this ocean of DIY vaporwave, labels serve as flagships for the most significant releases. They represent a guarantee of artistic quality similar to traditional indies like Flying Nun or Sub Pop. Of course, this being vaporwave, prominent imprints often bear corporate monikers such as Fortune 500 and Business Casual, names that gently satirize cult labels' brand value. Label underwriting of physical releases, in themselves a mark of prestige in vaporwave, is also important.

Vaporwave labels have their own aesthetics, too. "You can think of the vaporwave label, and you think of the music," Luke observes. "You know what you're getting under all these umbrellas." He believes that such aesthetics have affected the sound of different Eyeliner albums: "Coming into contact with the labels, something magic happens . . . deep converging." True, Beer on the Rug only became involved with *BUY NOW* late in the day. But given the early influence of Computer Dreams and other artists on Eyeliner, Luke's hunch was a good one. The album's shaded complexity fits well with the label's catalog.

Nevertheless, by February 2016, *BUY NOW* was no longer on Beer on the Rug. Luke transferred digital distribution over to his Bandcamp page. Here, the album still bore the Kansas label's imprimatur in the release notes (BOTR was, after all, a vaporwave touchstone). More consolidation was also underway on Luke's Bandcamp. Following CMR's shutdown in October 2015, he added Eyeliner's earlier releases along with the Disasteradio back catalog. Soon, most of his music could be downloaded from his Bandcamp on a pay-as-you-like basis.

Gauging an album's impact in the digital age is complex: streaming data, downloads, and physical sales all need to be factored in. Assessing critical reception is not simple either. The Internet's democratizing effects mean that evaluation of music is now diffused across online magazines, blogs, forums, ratings sites, and review aggregators, even at the granular level of user comments. This wealth of information offers rich ways of understanding how an album like *BUY NOW* is received, both on release and in the longer term. The Internet being a dynamic environment, what follows is a snapshot of Internet responses taken in August 2023, including content that had accrued since 2015.

For a niche indie album, *BUY NOW* enjoyed healthy sales in the first months after release. For several weeks on Bandcamp, possibly the Internet's largest direct-to-fan website, *BUY NOW* was among the best-selling albums tagged with either "vaporwave" or "New Zealand." The edition of 150 cassettes quickly sold out. But it didn't hit the New Zealand national charts, which did not account for Bandcamp sales until December 2016 and, after that, only of purchases by customers in New Zealand. However, traditional chart systems based on national territories seem less relevant for artists with globally dispersed followings like Eyeliner.

BUY NOW began receiving kudos in other ways. There were several early reviews in online magazines, the UK-based *Fact* placing the album among the best recent Bandcamp releases and praising Eyeliner's "knack for spinning . . . dated elements into welcomingly spacey funk."[5] *Tiny Mix Tapes*, a US webzine, published a review in the form of postmodern fiction whose characters find *BUY NOW* reminiscent of childhood vacations at some second-rate resort.[6] The webzine later published a more straightforward review in a quarterly roundup, pinpointing certain achievements:

> [While] Eyeliner has previously been about negotiating tacky, throwaway commercial samples and repackaging them, *Buy Now* has been pumped full of soul to give it an almost frightening feeling of sincerity. Each track is slick and refined, breathing new life into a musical era that grossly misread its own potential; the album's tangy overlap into modern dance music results in some wonderfully catchy melodies and heady buildups . . . No other album on this list will have been birthed from a musical style that sounds so "bad," and for that, *Buy Now* deserves a place as one of our unrivaled favorites.[7]

There was only sparse coverage in New Zealand. In July 2015, Zac Arnold interviewed Luke for public broadcaster Radio New Zealand. He raised the question of whether audiences

---

[5] Bowe 2015.
[6] C Monster 2015.
[7] Birkut 2015.

would fully grasp vaporwave's critical function beneath the nostalgia: "How the listener cannot necessarily understand when someone's critiquing economics or whether they're embracing the outcome of that economic structure."[8] Evaluated ideologically, Arnold implies, vaporwave seems dangerously ambiguous. Yet his observation also pays tribute to the artistry of BUY NOW's postironic balancing act.

In the online vaporwave scene, where Eyeliner was already recognized as a core artist, BUY NOW also garnered accolades. An end-of-year poll on the r/vaporwave subreddit placed the album 10th out of a field of 110. In late 2016, a larger opinion sample was taken for the *Vaporwave Essentials Guide Nu Edition*, covering releases from the 2014–16 period. Suggestions and votes were gathered from Reddit, 4Chan, 8Chan, Facebook, and other forums, and BUY NOW made the cut under the "Hypnagogic" subcategory.

Unofficial uploads provide another indication of the album's reception. Some of these even predate BUY NOW's release for streaming. On June 30, 2015, "Toy Dog" was uploaded to YouTube by the user Pan ja and has since received 29,000 views. The most significant upload was on Vapor Memory, a non-monetized YouTube channel dedicated to archiving notable albums (over 3,000 to date). Here, BUY NOW has racked up 272,973 views, 6,900 likes, 57 dislikes, and 443 comments.

The comments on the Vapor Memory upload are illuminating in several respects. As the 99 percent approval rating suggests, many users hold the album in high regard, with memories of 1980s–1990s period it evokes a recurring

---
[8] Arnold 2015.

theme. Some comments refer to the retro sounds of the Korg M1 and *Seinfeld* slap bass, but the most frequent references are to the soundtracks of games such as *SimCity* (1989), *Mario Paint* (1992), and *Shadowrun* (1994), and retro-styled examples like *Sonic Mania* (2017). The longest thread reminisces about *Kid Pix*, a drawing-animation program first released in 1989.[9] The computer game/software connections are significant, underlining how interaction with computers has been so formative for millennials and later generations, including software's musical accompaniments. The appreciative responses also tally with academic research pointing to vaporwave's "affective potential" for listeners,[10] even for those not born until the new millennium. According to this view, the way that vaporwave decontextualizes its musical sources creates a neutral openness of feeling that permits listeners to explore and form their own emotional connections.

BUY NOW's Bandcamp page also features mini-reviews from purchasers. In keeping with the website's interface, many name a favorite track ("Toy Dog" is currently the frontrunner). Similar content also appears on database websites such as Rate Your Music, where the album scores 3.27/5 from 640 ratings, and Discogs, where it scores 4.46/5 from 104 ratings. Given Discogs's other main function as a secondhand marketplace, the higher rating there potentially reflects the opinions of listeners who already own or are seeking a physical copy.

---

[9] Luke had not previously heard of *Kid Pix*.
[10] Killeen 2018.

Releases on cassettes and other vintage physical formats have been a feature of vaporwave from the start. It's a trend carried over from precursor genres such as hypnagogic pop and chillwave. Simon Reynolds argues that renewed interest in cassettes has been driven by nostalgia for the 1980s, a time when they were both a mass format and DIY medium.[11] He also notes the aesthetic appeal of cassettes' analog "warmth" in an age of bit-perfect digital audio. Such factors are relevant for vaporwave too, along with the sonic analogy between slowed-down samples and the characteristic stretched sound of overplayed tapes. By the time of *BUY NOW*'s 2015 release, cassettes were de rigueur for vaporwave label releases.

BUY NOW has subsequently been reissued in several formats by labels in New Zealand, the United States, and Canada. These reissues testify to the esteem in which the album has come to be held, with scarcity value being another factor: All the *BUY NOW* reissues have been limited to 500 copies or less, leaving the door open for future editions. Physical editions also hold appeal for variations that make them more collectible. On the first *BUY NOW* cassette, for instance, EyeBodega's design is more extensive than the digital artwork, spreading to both sides of the card liner and the yellow cassette shell. The *BUY NOW* face has also been altered to fit different media, often with an alternative version of the right eye. Physical editions also include information absent from digital download and streamed versions, notably that the album is dedicated to Luke's partner, Chloe, and their toy dog Ralph. There is now

---

[11] Reynolds 2011: 349–51.

a healthy secondary market for *BUY NOW*: on Discogs, some editions can change hands for several hundred dollars.

The first reissue of *BUY NOW* was on blue vinyl, released in 2018 on A Low Hum (500 copies, HUM057). By this time, vinyl records had themselves experienced a resurgence, an upturn dating to the late 2000s.[12] Factors driving demand are like those for cassettes, but vinyl, with its superior audio, larger packaging, and hefty price tag, is a luxury-grade format. The vinyl revival reached vaporwave in the mid-2010s when labels with the means started offering releases on both cassette and vinyl. Given vaporwave's interest in commodity culture, the idea of issuing products in several supposedly obsolete formats—catering to budget and deluxe markets—naturally resonates. Subsequent *BUY NOW* reissues push these ironies even further.

Next to reissue *BUY NOW* was the US electronic music label Midwest Collective (MWC), founded in Portland, Oregon, in 2013. First up was a 2020 pressing on yellow vinyl (500 copies, MWC056LP). Luke also prepared a Deluxe Edition with four bonus tracks from the *BUY NOW* preproduction period: "Bon Appétit," "Body Glove," "British Open," and "Magic Eye." MWC issued this version as a purple cassette (450 copies, MWC056MC), while Luke made it available digitally through Bandcamp. Then, in 2021, they issued the Deluxe Edition as part of a triple-MiniDisc set, *Eyeliner MiniDisc Day Collection 2021* (60 copies, MWC-056-MD), also containing the two CMR albums. MiniDisc was a format launched by Sony in 1992, mainly for home recording. Although gaining followings in Japan and

---

[12] Bartmanski and Woodward 2015: 26–8.

Europe, the format had mediocre commercial success and Sony discontinued the technology in 2013. To reissue an album on MiniDisc in 2021 takes the love of obsolete formats to a new level, and the *Eyeliner Collection* may live on as one of the few triple sets ever released.

BUY NOW has since come out in yet another archaic format. This 2023 edition was issued by the Canadian label Strudelsoft on a 3.5-inch floppy disk (75 copies, STR-048). Holding around 1.44 MB, such disks were once a standard data-storage format—and a very minor music format, a handful coming out with audio, interactive media, MIDI, or screensavers, sometimes accompanying a standard CD (the most prominent instance being Billy Idol's 1993 album *Cyberpunk*). In the 2010s there was renewed interest from underground artists. Unsurprisingly, given the genre's predilections, vaporwave floppy disk releases started early, the first being Miami Vice's *Culture Island* (2012).[13] The Strudelsoft edition of *BUY NOW* consists of MIDI files exported from Luke's Nuendo sessions. Hearing these files requires an application with sound-font capabilities such as Windows Media Player. While the Strudelsoft Bandcamp download also includes MP3s rendered using default sounds, these MIDI files hold many other possibilities, more on which below.

If *BUY NOW*'s physical reissues reflect its high reputation with hardcore vaporwave fans, then the album's performance on music streaming platforms provides a bigger picture. Streaming—continuous playback of digital music over the

---

[13] Weingarten 2018.

Internet—became a viable distribution model in the late 2000s. Bandwidth had increased enough by then to make these services technically feasible. The music industry was also seeking alternatives to downloads, given ongoing difficulties with unauthorized file-sharing. Streaming took off. Subscription and ad-supported streaming now account for 67 percent of global music industry revenue.[14]

Shortly after its Bandcamp release, *BUY NOW* became available on most platforms, Spotify proving by far the most significant, followed by Apple Music and YouTube. Spotify's public interface provides some information about the ongoing popularity of tracks and artists, with further analytics available to artists so they can better understand their audiences. Because of the insights it provides, Luke made his data available for this book in August 2023, eight years after streaming of *BUY NOW* began.

Between 2015 and 2023, *BUY NOW*'s tracks were collectively streamed over 5 million times on Spotify. "Pinot Noir" makes up 35 percent of streams, "Toy Dog" 23.5 percent. The album accounts for over 60 percent of Eyeliner's total streams. Information about the locations and demographics of listeners, and how they found and interacted with tracks, is available only for the entire Eyeliner catalog. Eyeliner's audience is dispersed globally, but unevenly: around 56 percent of listeners are in the United States, with 64 percent in North America as a whole. By contrast, only 20 percent of Spotify's 551 million users are in North America.[15] Eyeliner has

---
[14] IFPI 2023: 11.
[15] "Q2 2023 Update."

its largest Spotify audiences in US cities such as Los Angeles, Chicago, Atlanta, and Portland (Oregon), a municipality known for its vaporwave activity. Considering vaporwave's themes, it's perhaps unsurprising that Eyeliner does such brisk business in the cradle of consumer culture. Audiences in Canada, United Kingdom, Australia, Brazil, and Germany also figure highly. New Zealand has the eighteenth-highest national audience (0.7 percent), although on a per-capita basis, it's fourth highest behind the United States, Canada, and Finland, suggesting ongoing awareness of Luke's work in his home country.

US-market data from 2020 (the most recent available) suggests that gen-Z and millennials comprise around two-thirds of Spotify's users, with gen-X and older users making up the remainder.[16] Eyeliner's audience by contrast skews more heavily toward millennials (around 50 percent) and gen-Z (44 percent). Can Eyeliner's Spotify audience be assumed as synonymous with vaporwave's broader fanbase? If so, the data confirms the genre appeals most to those with childhoods in the 1980s to early 2000s period.

Spotify also includes user-generated content in the form of favorites, libraries, and playlists. Eyeliner has over 12,000 Spotify followers with tracks being added to almost 165,000 playlists and libraries. Playlists are the originating source for most Eyeliner streams, with support from aficionados playing a major role. The single most important playlist is "Vaporwave" (started in 2014 by the user After Eating), featuring six *BUY NOW* tracks. It was the source of 11 percent of all Eyeliner streams between 2018 and 2023. But Spotify's own editorial

---

[16] Email from Kate Perry (Spotify Australia-New Zealand), September 2, 2023.

playlists, radio, and algorithms have also led many people to the album. Together, these were the sources of 30 percent of Eyeliner streams.

Spotify has also been financially significant for Luke. In a 2022 article on the *Stuff* news website, he disclosed that payments from the platform had reached a level sufficient "to pay for his weekly grocery shop."[17] These payments are currently his largest source of music revenue, topped up with less-regular Bandcamp sales. *BUY NOW* accounts for the bulk of this income.

The royalty rates Spotify allocates independent musicians are the subject of ongoing debate and criticism.[18] Luke himself regards them as inadequate, but being an indie solo artist has advantages. As he retains all music rights, none of the streaming income is siphoned off to a record company, nor does Luke need to split it with bandmates or songwriting partners. He can take home 100 percent of the Spotify pie, such as is given.

To put Eyeliner's streaming further into perspective, one can compare it with that of Disasteradio. In Disasteradio's prime period, Luke grew a national audience through live gigs and student radio. This approach worked to the extent that Disasteradio remains his most identifiable artist brand in New Zealand. But such local recognition counts for less online compared with becoming a profiled artist in a cult genre. Eyeliner currently makes up over 96 percent of all Luke's Spotify streams, with a rolling average

---
[17] Smith 2022.
[18] Giblin and Doctorow 2022: 66–77.

of around 41,000 monthly listeners (roughly the same as local contemporaries TrinityRoots). By contrast, Disasteradio manages around 600.

Luke's ongoing commitment to making his music freely available fits surprisingly well into the streaming economy. He has always wanted his music to circulate widely, and the early 2000s file-sharing practices that so infuriated musicians such as Metallica's Lars Ulrich were a boon for indie artists like him. Since its release, *BUY NOW* has generally been available from Bandcamp on a pay-as-you-like basis, although he currently charges a nominal US$2.00 for the Deluxe Edition. In any case, you don't need to buy *BUY NOW*: the album can be freely downloaded from vaporwave archives in the Internet Archive and elsewhere. That people are now willing to subscribe to Spotify for its convenience or purchase physical editions has only strengthened Luke's belief in an open-access model. It turns out that many people have been willing to stump up for *BUY NOW* even under Bandcamp's voluntary payment option.

Has music offered financial independence, though? No. Luke has always needed day jobs and freelance contracts to support himself financially. "My inability to earn a living [from music] drives me crazy," he acknowledges. Still, despite the precarity of indie distribution, he believes a more traditional industry career would have been even less fruitful. "If I had involved myself with a label where I don't own the rights and I don't own the back catalog," he figures, "I'd be in a worse position." The road taken may yet reap future dividends. Luke continues to pick up occasional soundtrack work and *BUY NOW* is the perfect freelancer's portfolio.

An independent mindset may be hardwired in any case. Combined with the pay-as-you-like model, Luke has also long released his music under Creative Commons licenses. Established in 2002, the Creative Commons (CC) system enables creative works to be copied and shared without further approval from copyright holders, some licenses also permitting reuse and remixing.[19] CC is now used extensively on the Internet, applying, for instance, to all Wikipedia articles. Trent Reznor of Nine Inch Nails is among the more well-known proponents in the music world.

Since adopting Creative Commons licensing in 2006, Luke has tended to apply the same license to his recordings. While the music can be freely shared, it needs to be attributed to him (BY), used only non-commercially (NC), and any new works that sample or remix it must be "shared alike" (SA), that is, made available under the same BY-NC-SA license. He has long been a supporter of sampling and remix culture. "I believe I have a responsibility to allow my peers to sample my work," he stated in 2010. "I'd feel guilty if I wasn't 'putting something in the pot' so to speak."[20] At the same time, the license reserves his commercial rights, with financial exploitation of any derivative works requiring further negotiation.

Luke released *BUY NOW* under the BY-NC-SA license, opening its potential for reuse within days by posting a MediaFire download link to stems for "Toy Dog" on Reddit. A comprehensive set of production materials became downloadable in May 2021 through the Turnbull Library's

---
[19] Lessig 2004.
[20] "Case Study: Luke Rowell."

digital archive. To publicize the Turnbull project, an offshoot album was released on Bandcamp, *Free: Buy Now Remixes* (2021), showcasing the possibilities of Creative Commons with fourteen remixes of *BUY NOW* tracks by artists from the United States, United Kingdom, Sweden, and New Zealand. What "remix" denotes here varies widely. Some artists took MIDI and assigned different VST instruments; others chopped, looped, or otherwise edited audio stems. MIDI was sometimes adapted to new rhythms, with many tracks adding samples and new instrumental parts. The overall results attest to *BUY NOW*'s strong compositions, robust enough to be reconfigured in any number of electronic music styles, including drum and bass, dub, and ambient. Several remixes were later reissued elsewhere, with the Turnbull archive being downloaded to create more remixes posted to Bandcamp and YouTube.[21]

Nor would a tale of Internet-age music be complete without a little unauthorized sampling. In March 2021, the song "Soul Searchin'" by Jenniva, a New York R&B singer, was uploaded to YouTube. It featured a prominent sample from "Pinot Noir," which she had purchased through a beat market website where it was being offered without Luke's authorization. While exemplifying the Internet's scope for piracy, "Soul Searchin'" also represents more kudos for the sleek riff that powers *BUY NOW*'s most streamed track. After Luke learned about the song, he and Jenniva reached an understanding, and the track remains online.[22]

---

[21] Brown 2021, 2022.
[22] Pepperell 2021.

In retrospect, *BUY NOW* came out at a pivotal time for vaporwave. The scene has greatly expanded since 2015. The r/vaporwave subreddit, for example, which Luke joined during its first month of existence, had reached 14,000 members by the time of *BUY NOW*'s release. It was only just getting started. New subscriptions climbed steeply and, as of December 2023, membership stands at over 283,000. As noted in the Introduction, the year 2016 saw an explosion in the number of new Bandcamp releases; eight years later, over 40,000 releases tagged "vaporwave" are available on the site. The Internet Archive's Vapor Vault contains a similar amount. Wider interest in the genre also took off in the mid-2010s, with Google searches for the term "vaporwave" almost quadrupling between June 2015 and December 2016. Critics began perceiving its influence on mainstream artists such as Ariane Grande and Drake.[23] The first book about vaporwave, *Babbling Corpse*, was published in 2016, along with the first academic coverage.[24] Inevitably, vaporwave's visual aesthetic has also been co-opted back into corporate advertising, including for the "dream flavored" Coca-Cola released in 2022. The genre keeps dying and showing yet more signs of life.

BUY NOW likely benefited from appearing on the cusp of this new phase. The album continues to be discovered and acclaimed by new aficionados, a prominent example being the YouTuber known as Pad Chennington. Since 2017, Chennington has created hundreds of vaporwave video guides and reviews, accruing almost 10 million views. *BUY*

---

[23] Beauchamp 2016; Nordin 2020.
[24] Tanner 2016; Trainer 2016.

NOW is featured in "107 Vaporwave Albums You Should Know!" (2018), and Chennington later rated it among twenty-four "classics of the classics" for "Vaporwave Albums Tier List" (2022).

Debates about the genre's meaning and scope rumbled on after 2012, as the scene has slowly evolved into something a bit more conventional, with live festivals, many artists dispensing with anonymity, and more emphasis on aesthetics than ideological critique. Yet the term "vaporwave" remains the anchor point for an expanding fleet of adjacent styles. In this context, *BUY NOW* has aged well. The album's sonic diversity and funkiness can be appreciated from multiple angles, while the all-original MIDI approach that Eyeliner used from the start has also spread, adopted by prominent artists including FM Skyline and Windows96.

Back in Wellington, the Skyranch era came to an end in 2016 when its building was demolished to make way for new earthquake-compliant apartments. Luke moved on and Disasteradio returned, *Sweatshop* finally coming out the following year. He had been plugging away at this synthpop homecoming for seven years. In contrast with *BUY NOW*'s sweetly ambivalent riff on consumerism, *Sweatshop* is more outspoken. Most barbed is the title track, concerning the factories run by Taiwanese company Foxconn, the world's largest technology manufacturer, including for brands such as Apple, Kindle, Nintendo, Cisco, Microsoft, and Sony. In 2010, Foxconn reportedly installed netting on the exteriors of its plants to prevent suicides by workers driven to desperation by harsh conditions.

Eyeliner's next album came out in 2020. *Drop Shadow*, released by Ohio-based label Orange Milk Records, continued the exploration of ambient-new age from "Pictionary," with side studies in dance music and TV themes. The follow-up, *brb*, was issued by My Pet Flamingo in November 2023. Composed while Luke was living in Hong Kong in 2020–22, the title is an abbreviation ("be right back") from the early IRC chat-room days. Infusing classic Eyeliner compositions with a tropical vibe, *brb* became a best-selling "New Zealand" and "vaporwave"-tagged album on Bandcamp for several weeks (even briefly ranking fifth in overall Bandcamp sales). The attention also led to *BUY NOW* bubbling up among "New Zealand"-tagged Bandcamp bestsellers, eight years after its initial release.

Conclusion

For audience response, critical accolades, and community respect, *BUY NOW* is Luke Rowell's leading album to date. Even as vaporwave has evolved over a decade, the album's exuberance and originality have kept it fresh. *BUY NOW* is a vaporwave—and a New Zealand—classic.

On many levels, the album is a product of the digital revolution and the Internet age, including the VST technology used (and the earlier technologies that this recreates) and the networked environment of Web 2.0. But real-world context and timing also left their traces, *BUY NOW* marking the moment when Luke mastered the compositional approaches he'd been teaching himself for years and was stretching out into new territory. Freelance work making advertising music was another prime catalyst, enabling him to ironically—and sincerely—reflect upon this professional work while moonlighting as Eyeliner. *BUY NOW* sprang from a period of heightened double consciousness.

BUY NOW is also a high point in an excavation of the musical past that goes back to early Disasteradio. Rummaging among forgotten genres of previous decades, *BUY NOW* reveals a wealth of overlooked beauty, while not forgetting that such cultural capital came—and still comes—at a cost. Vaporwave is the music of a generation coming to terms with the contradictions of the world they have grown up in, finding a way through, and producing art that acknowledges this complexity. But it's also a world we all inhabit. Time to succumb to the sales pitch again and take a sip of *BUY NOW*'s vaporwave elixir.

References

"2016: The Year in Stats" (2016), *Bandcamp Daily*: https://daily.bandcamp.com/lists/2016-the-year-in-stats (accessed December 1, 2022).

"Adam Smith's Islands" (1988), *The Economist*, March 5: 70–1.

Allen-Robertson, J. (2013), *Digital Culture Industry*, New York: Palgrave Macmillan.

Arnett, R. (2020), *Neo-Noir as Post-Classical Hollywood Cinema*, Cham: Springer International Publishing.

Arnold, Z. (2015), "Eyeliner—Buy Now," *Radio New Zealand*: https://www.rnz.co.nz/national/programmes/nat-music/audio/201761112/eyeliner-buy-now (accessed March 29, 2023).

Bartmanski, D. and I. Woodward (2015), *Vinyl: The Analogue Record in the Digital Age*, New York: Routledge.

Battino, D. (1995), "20 Sounds that Must Die!," *Keyboard*, October: 65-74.

Beauchamp, S. (2016), "How Vaporwave was Created then Destroyed by the Internet," *Esquire*: https://www.esquire.com/entertainment/music/a47793/what-happened-to-vaporwave/ (accessed April 24, 2023).

Bennett, A. (2013), "Cheesy Listening: Popular Music and Ironic Listening Practices," in S. Baker, A. Bennett, and J. Taylor (eds.), *Redefining Mainstream Popular Music*, 202–13, New York: Routledge.

Birkut (2015), "2015: Third Quarter Favorites," *Tiny Mix Tapes*: https://www.tinymixtapes.com/features/2015-third-quarter-favorites (accessed August 23, 2023).

Blink [I. Jorgenson] (2004), "Disasteradio," *A Low Hum*, 8: 28–30.

Bodinger-deUriarte, C. (1985), "Opposition to Hegemony in the Music of Devo: A Simple Matter of Remembering," *Journal of Popular Culture*, 18 (4): 57–71.

Born, G. and C. Haworth (2018), "From Microsound to Vaporwave: Internet-Mediated Musics, Online Methods, and Genre," *Music & Letters*, 98 (4): 601–47.

Bowe, M. (2015), "Name Your Price: June's Best Bandcamp Releases," *Fact*: https://www.factmag.com/2015/07/02/name-your-price-junes-best-bandcamp-releases/ (accessed August 23, 2023).

Brown, M. (2021), "Download Now… Free!" *National Library of New Zealand*: https://natlib.govt.nz/blog/posts/download-now-free (accessed August 31, 2023).

Brown, M. (2022), "The Disasteradio Project," *National Library of New Zealand*: https://natlib.govt.nz/blog/posts/the-disasteradio-project (accessed August 31, 2023).

Burgess, R. (2014), *The History of Music Production*, Oxford: Oxford University Press.

Burns, P. (1989), *Fatal Success: A History of the New Zealand Company*, Auckland: Heinemann Reed.

C Monster (2015), "Eyeliner—Buy Now," *Tiny Mix Tapes*: https://www.tinymixtapes.com/music-review/eyeliner-buy-now (accessed August 23, 2023).

"Case Study: Luke Rowell" (2010), *Creative Commons Aotearoa New Zealand* (archived March 14, 2010): https://web.archive.org/web/20100314013011/http://www.creativecommons.org.nz/creative_commoners/luke_rowell_disasteradio (accessed March 23, 2023).

Chennington, P. (2019), "The 'Perfect' Music Genre? (Utopian Virtual)," *YouTube*: https://www.youtube.com/watch?v=TPxqFxGRPxM (accessed December 4, 2022).

Cole, R. (2020), "Vaporwave Aesthetics: Internet Nostalgia and the Utopian Impulse," *ASAP/Journal*, 5 (2): 297–326.

Collins, K. (2008), *Game Sound*, Cambridge: Massachusetts Institute of Technology.

Corbett, S. (2014), "Stuck in the Middle," *This American Life*: https://www.thisamericanlife.org/516/stuck-in-the-middle-2014 (accessed July 10, 2023).

deliriously...daniel (2019), "Projected Runways: Sharing the Fashionwave Fantasy," *Private Suite*, 7: 44–53.

Dellinger, J. and D. Giffels (2003), *Are We Not Men? We are Devo!*, London: SAF Publishing.

Dettmar, K. (2013), *Is Rock Dead?* New York: Routledge.

Dowd, T. (2013), "Music from Abroad: The Internationalization of the US Mainstream Music Market, 1940–1990," in S. Baker, A. Bennett, and J. Taylor (eds.), *Redefining Mainstream Popular Music*, 125–36, New York: Routledge.

Duffy, B. (2021), *Generations: Does When You're Born Shape Who You Are?* London: Atlantic Books.

Dunleavy, T. (2005), *Ourselves in Primetime: A History of New Zealand Television Drama*, Auckland: Auckland University Press.

Emmerling, C. (2020), "Seinfeld," *Twenty Thousand Hertz*: https://www.20k.org/episodes/seinfeld (accessed May 10, 2023).

Fantano, A. (2012), "Macintosh Plus—Floral Shoppe ALBUM REVIEW," *YouTube*: https://www.youtube.com/watch?v=f0D9lyyeEEU (accessed November 29, 2023).

Galil, L. (2013), "Vaporwave and the Observer Effect," *Chicago Reader*: https://chicagoreader.com/music/vaporwave-and-the-observer-effect/ (accessed March 29, 2023).

Galt, M. (2022), "Reflections on Not in Narrow Seas: The Economic History of Aotearoa New Zealand 1," *Journal of New Zealand Studies*, 34: 87–93.

Giblin, R. and C. Doctorow (2022), *Chokepoint Capitalism,* Carlton North: Scribe.

Girls Blood (2012), "Vaporwave Essentials," *Girls Blood*: https://www.girlsblood.com/2012/11/vaporwave-essentials.html (accessed April 14, 2023).

Glitsos, L. (2018), "Vaporwave, or Music Optimised for Abandoned Malls," *Popular Music*, 37 (1): 100–18.

Gooding, S. (2018), "Scene Report: The New Zealand Artists Taking Vaporwave in New Directions," *Bandcamp Daily*: https://daily.bandcamp.com/scene-report/new-zealand-vaporwave-list (accessed June 7, 2023).

Goodwin, A. (1992), "Rationalization and Democratization in the New Technologies of Popular Music," in J. Lull (ed.), *Popular Music and Communication*, 2nd edn, 75–100, Newbury Park: Sage.

Hara, K. (2020), *Joe Hisaishi's Soundtrack for My Neighbor Totoro*, London: Bloomsbury Academic.

Hardwick, M. J. (2004), *Mall Maker: Victor Gruen, Architect of an American Dream*, Philadelphia: University of Pennsylvania Press.

Harper, A. (2012a), "Vaporwave and the Pop-Art of the Virtual Plaza," *Dummy*: https://www.dummymag.com/news/adam-harper-vaporwave/ (accessed September 23, 2022).

Harper, A. (2012b), "Isn't It Ironic?" *Dummy*: https://dmy.co/news/essay-isn-t-it-ironic (accessed March 27, 2023).

Harper, A. (2013a), "Invest in Vaporwave Futures!" *Dummy*: https://dmy.co/features/essay-invest-in-vaporwave-futures (accessed March 28, 2023).

Harper, A. (2013b), "Some Chillwave Differences," *Rouge's Foam*: https://rougesfoam.blogspot.com/2013/08/some-chillwave-differences.html (accessed March 28, 2023).

Harper, A. (2013c), "Pattern Recognition Vol. 8.5: The Year in Vaporwave," *Electronic Beats*: https://www.electronicbeats.net/vol-8-5-the-year-in-vaporwave/ (accessed April 20, 2023)

Harper, A. (2014), "Bridging the Streams," *The Wire*, January: 41.

Hibbett, R. (2010), "The New Age Taboo," *Journal of Popular Music Studies,* 22 (3): 283–308.

Hillary Commission (1991), *Life in New Zealand Survey Commission Report Volume IV: Leisure*, Wellington: Hillary Commission.

Holloway-Smith, B. (n.d.), "Pioneer City (2010–2XXX)," *Bronwyn Holloway-Smith*: https://hollowaysmith.nz/pioneer-city/#id2 (accessed March 23, 2023).

IFPI [International Federation of the Phonographic Industry] (2023), "Global Music Report 2023," *IFPI*: https://www.ifpi.org/wp-content/uploads/2020/03/Global_Music_Report_2023_State_of_the_Industry.pdf (accessed August 29, 2023).

Kearns, R., L. Murphy, and W. Friesen (2001), "Shopping!" in C. Bell (ed.), *Sociology of Everyday Life in New Zealand*, 189–209, Palmerston North: Dunmore Press.

Kilby, D. (2017), "Guide to Vaporwave Guides," *Sunbleach*: https://sunbleach.net/2017/12/02/feature-guide-to-vaporwave-guides/ (accessed April 14, 2023).

Killeen, P. (2018), "Burned Out Myths and Vapour Trails: Vaporwave's Affective Potentials," *Open Cultural Studies,* 2: 626–38.

Kim, T. (2020), "Accelerationism and Techno-Orientalism in Macintosh Plus's Floral Shoppe," *The Macksey Journal*, 1: article 209.

Klein, N. (2001), *No Logo*, London: Flamingo.

Konstantinou, L. (2016), *Cool Characters: Irony and American Fiction*, Cambridge: Harvard University Press.

Konstantinou, L. (2017), "Four Faces of Postirony," in R. van den Akker, A. Gibbons, and T. Vermeulen (eds.), *Metamodernism: Historicity, Affect, and Depth after Postmodernism*, 87–102, London: Rowman & Littlefield.

Lanza, J. (1994), *Elevator Music*, New York: Picador.

Lavengood, M. (2019), "What Makes It Sound '80s?: The Yamaha DX7 Electric Piano Sound," *Journal of Popular Music Studies*, 31 (3): 73–94.

Leight, E. (2023), "The Tidal Wave of New 'Songs,'" *Billboard*, February 25: 25–6.

Leppert, A. (2019), *TV Family Values: Gender, Domestic Labor, and 1980s Sitcoms*, New Brunswick: Rutgers University Press.

LeRoy, D. (2023), *Dancing to the Drum Machine: How Electronic Percussion Conquered the World*, New York: Bloomsbury Academic.

Leslie, J. (2007), "Larry Graham: Trunk of the Funk Tree," *Bass Player*, May: 30–7.

Lessig, L. (2004), *Free Culture*, London: Penguin Press.

Levy, A. (1966), "Telephone Hold Program System," *United States Patent Office*: https://patents.google.com/patent/US3246082 (accessed July 7, 2023).

Manning, P. (2013), *Electronic and Computer Music*, 4th edn, Oxford: Oxford University Press.

Newman, K. (2008), *Connecting the Clouds: The Internet in New Zealand*, Auckland: Activity Press.

Nordin, I. (2020), "Vaporwave Might Be Dead, But Its Ghost Continues to Haunt Pop Music," *Study Breaks*: https://studybreaks.com/culture/music/vaporwave-ghost-influence/ (accessed November 1, 2023).

Pepperell, M. (2021), "Disasteradio," *AudioCulture*: https://www.audioculture.co.nz/profile/disasteradio (accessed September 23, 2022).

Prensky, M. (2001), "Digital Natives, Digital Immigrants Part 1," *On the Horizon,* 9 (5): 1–6.

Purves, A. and W. Elley (1994), "The Role of the Home and Student Differences in Reading Performance," in W. Elley (ed.), *The IEA Study of Reading Literacy: Achievement and Instruction in Thirty-Two School Systems,* 89–121, New York: Pergamon.

"Q2 2023 Update" (2023), *Spotify:* https://s29.q4cdn.com/175625835/files/doc_financials/2023/q2/Shareholder-Deck-Q2-2023-FINAL.pdf (accessed December 13, 2023).

"Revenant Forms: The Meaning of Hauntology" (2010), *The Wire:* https://www.thewire.co.uk/audio/in-conversation/the-wire-salon_revenant-forms_the-meaning-of-hauntology (accessed December 1, 2023).

Reynolds, S. (2011), *Retromania,* London: Faber and Faber.

Rivers, P. (2018), "New Jack Swing," in T. Riggs (ed.), *St. James Encyclopedia of Hip Hop Culture,* 316–18, Farmington Hills: St. James Press.

Robinson, J. (2015), *The Oxford Companion to Wine,* 4th edn, Oxford: Oxford University Press.

Rowell, L. (2017), "[VST08] Eyeliner," *Reddit:* https://www.reddit.com/r/makingvaporwave/comments/5od2t6/vst08_eyeliner/ (accessed May 18, 2023).

Rowell, L. and S. Ward (2015), "Eyeliner—'Buy Now'—NEW ALBUM JUNE 27 2015," *YouTube:* https://www.youtube.com/watch?v=2Rl5ZANdwAo (accessed November 3, 2021).

Serres, M. (2015), *Thumbelina: The Culture and Technology of Millennials,* trans. D. Smith, London: Rowman & Littlefield.

Shaviro, S. (2006). "Prophecies of the Present," *Socialism & Democracy,* 20 (3): 5–24.

Shute, G. (2014), "A Low Hum—Part 1," *AudioCulture:* https://www.audioculture.co.nz/articles/a-low-hum-part-1 (accessed September 30, 2022)

Shute, G. (2023), "The Billion Streamers," *AudioCulture*: https://www.audioculture.co.nz/articles/the-billion-streamers (accessed September 29, 2023).

Situationist International Anthology (2006), rev. edn, ed. and trans. K. Knabb, Berkeley: Bureau of Public Secrets.

Smith, D. (2022), "As Neil Young Boycotts Spotify, Local Artists Struggle to Earn Royalties From Platform," *Stuff*: https://www.stuff.co.nz/business/127736174/as-neil-young-boycotts-spotify-local-artists-struggle-to-earn-royalties-from-platform (accessed August 30, 2023).

Smith, E. (2014), "Crystal Magic," *Radio New Zealand*: https://www.rnz.co.nz/national/programmes/nat-music/audio/2602279/crystal-magic (accessed April 24, 2023).

Smithies, G. (2011), "Out From Under the Radar," *Stuff*: http://www.stuff.co.nz/entertainment/music/5601379/Out-from-under-the-radar (accessed September 27, 2022).

Sontag, S. (1966), *Against Interpretation*, New York: Farrar, Straus & Giroux.

Stahl, G. (2018), "Urban Melancholy: Tales from Wellington's Music Scene," in S. Brunt and G. Stahl (eds.), *Made in Australia and Aotearoa/New Zealand*, 121–30, New York: Routledge.

Steely Dan—Aja: Classic Albums (1999), [DVD] Dir. A. Lewens, Rajonvision RV0490.

Taylor, T. D. (2012), *The Sounds of Capitalism: Advertising, Music, and the Conquest of Culture*, Chicago: University of Chicago Press.

Taylor, T. D. (2016), *Music and Capitalism: A History of the Present*, Chicago: University of Chicago Press.

Tenzer, M. (2019), "That's All It Does: Steve Reich and Balinese Gamelan," in S. Gopinath and P. Siôn (eds.), *Rethinking Reich*, 303–23, New York: Oxford University Press.

Thomas, M. (2017), "The Mixtape: Luke Rowell," *Radio New Zealand*: https://www.rnz.co.nz/news/the-wireless/374432/the-mixtape-luke-rowell (accessed June 20, 2022).

Trainer, A. (2016), "From Hypnagogia to Distroid: Postironic Musical Renderings of Personal Memory," in S. Whiteley and S. Rambarran (eds.), *The Oxford Handbook of Music and Virtuality*, 409–27, Oxford: Oxford University Press.

Vail, M. (2002), "Korg M1 (Retrozone)," *Sound on Sound*, February: https://www.soundonsound.com/reviews/korg-m1-retrozone (accessed May 10, 2023).

Warnett, G. (2016), "How Run-DMC Earned Their Adidas Stripes," *Mr Porter*: https://www.mrporter.com/en-nz/journal/lifestyle/how-run-dmc-earned-their-adidas-stripes-826882 (accessed June 26, 2023).

Weingarten, C. (2018), "Revolution at 3.5": Inside Vaporwave's Mini-Boom of Floppy Disk Releases," *Rolling Stone*: https://www.rollingstone.com/pro/features/vaporwave-floppy-disk-trend-666085/ (accessed August 25, 2023).

Whelan, A. (2017), "The Emergence of Vernacular Digital Music Cultures," in G. Goggin and M. McLelland (eds.), *The Routledge Companion to Global Internet Histories*, 436–47, New York: Routledge.

Whelan, A. (2020), "'Do You Have a Moment to Talk About Vaporwave?' Technology, Memory, and Critique in the Writing on an Online Music Scene," in T. Tofalvy and E. Barna (eds.), *Popular Music, Technology, and the Changing Media Ecosystem*, 185–200, Cham: Palgrave Macmillan.

Windsor, W. L. and C. de Bézenac (2012), "Music and Affordances," *Musicae Scientiae*, 16 (1): 102–20.

Yabsley, A. and E. Davoren-Britton (2014), "Genre Cult Episode 2—Vaporwave," *Gaming Cult*: https://archive.org/details/GENRECULTPODCASTEP2Vaporwave (accessed October 5, 2023).

Young, T. (1994), "The End of Irony?" *Modern Review*, April–May: 6–7.

Index

accelerationism   8, 43–4, 46
advertising   2, 36–8, 52, 53, 82, 87–8, 127
advertising music   1, 3, 18, 32, 38, 39, 42, 87, 89
   changes in 1980s–1990s   68–70, 101–2
   endorsement deals   69–70, 82
   musicians and producers   72, 75–7, 88
Alexander Turnbull Library   12
Altered Zones   34, 35, 45
Amazon.com   82, 111
ambient music   105–8, 126, 129
artificial intelligence (AI)   1, 74
Austin, Fraser   39, 51, 110

baby boomers   48, 69
background music   39, 46, 69, 75
Bandcamp   4, 45, 49, 111, 114, 120, 121, 127, 129
   Luke Rowell account   27, 112–14, 119, 126

Beer on the Rug   2, 34, 110–14
Burnett, Robin (INTERNET CLUB)   3, 7, 43, 44, 46
BUY NOW (album)
   "Chit Chat"   101–3, 105
   core music ingredients   60–6
   cover artwork   2, 111–12, 118
   critical reception   114–17, 127–8
   eclecticism of   1, 68–70
   editions and reissues   1–2, 111, 118–20
   "High Heels"   2, 87–9
   jazz influence on   62, 73–4, 76
   making of   54–5, 57–8, 60–6, 68–78
   "Payphone"   74, 89–92, 99, 100
   "Pictionary"   2, 105–8, 129
   "Pinot Noir"   2, 85–7, 103, 121, 126
   postironic sensibility of   63–6, 72, 116, 131

"Private Hospital" 73, 103–5
R&B influence on 62–3, 73, 78
release of 109–14
remixes of tracks 125–6
sales and revenue 112, 114–15, 118–19, 123–4, 129
"Showbiz" 95–8, 103
"Sneakers for Men" 2, 82–4, 87–8
streaming audiences 120–3
television influence on 1, 60–1, 68, 129
title of 95, 109–11
"Toy Dog" 79–82, 95, 102, 103, 116, 117, 121, 125
"Venetian Blinds" 2, 92–5, 104
"Windchimes" 74, 98–100

camp sensibility 16, 23, 28, 40, 53, 65, 72, 80, 81
capitalism 3–4, 20–1, 53–4, 76, 111; *see also* vaporwave
and sweatshops 82, 128
Commodore 64 16–17, 29
Computer Dreams 34, 35, 41–3, 110, 113
computer games 16–17, 20, 25, 26, 28, 98, 106–8, 117

consumerism 2–4, 7, 10, 43, 93, 111; *see also* advertising; shopping malls
and luxury 79–80, 112, 119
in New Zealand 21–2
and popular music 68–70, 82, 101
Creative Commons 11, 13, 27, 125–6
Crystal Magic Records 39, 45, 49–51, 109–10, 114, 119
Cudby, Chris 30, 39 n.6

Destination Pioneer City 37–9
détournement 36, 40, 44, 47, 52, 111
Devo 9, 23, 28, 32, 101
digital audio workstations (DAWs) 58–60, 73, 76; *see also* Nuendo
Disasteradio 5, 6, 28–32, 34, 45
Charisma 30, 31, 33, 34, 38, 60
Datasette 112
"Gravy Rainbow" 30, 32, 41
live performances 29–30, 50–1, 97
music distribution 112–14
music style 28–30
origin of name 28
on streaming services 123–4

Sweatshop 38, 128
Visions 30, 58
drum machines 7, 57, 64, 74–6, 83; *see also* LinnDrum
Dummy 42, 45, 46

EyeBodega 111, 118
Eyeliner
   brb 129
   compared to Disasteradio 30–2, 38–9, 52–3, 104
   Drop Shadow 128–9
   High Fashion Mood Music 3, 33, 39–42, 44–6, 48, 53, 60, 110
   LARP of Luxury 3, 51, 52, 55, 60, 68, 78, 86
   live performances 50
   and MIDI 3, 12, 59–60, 77, 128
   origin of name 40
   persona 40, 52–3, 66–8, 74, 84
   and postirony 41, 67, 70
   vaporwave style 3, 38–9, 46, 51–2, 66–8, 128

Ferraro, James 6–7, 42, 43, 46
   Far Side Virtual 35–6, 39, 51–2, 68
4Chan 3, 41, 44, 47, 116

generations; *see* baby boomers; generation X; generation Z; millennials
generation X (gen-X) 12, 122
generation Y; *see* millennials
generation Z (gen-Z) 10, 117, 122
Global Financial Crisis (GFC) 50, 54–5, 97, 104

Harper, Adam 3–4, 7–8, 42–7, 49, 51, 67
hip-hop 51 n.31, 82–3
Hisaishi, Joe 98–100
hold music 1, 68, 89–92, 99
Holloway-Smith, Bronwyn 37, 52

Internet
   advent of 12, 16, 21, 24–5
   impact on music 1, 11–12, 57, 109, 114
   IRC (Internet relay chat) 26–7, 129
   music distribution 1, 11, 109, 112 (*see also* Bandcamp; MP3.com; Napster; Spotify; YouTube)
music genres 2, 34–5
music streaming 1, 109, 113, 120–1, 124

and New Zealand music   5–6
Web 2.0   34–5, 41, 45, 47, 49, 131
websites (see *Altered Zones*; Amazon.com; *Dummy*; 4Chan; Reddit; *Rose Quartz*; Tumblr)
irony   3, 8–10, 32, 46, 65, 80, 101

Jeskola Buzz   25–7, 58, 59
Jorgenson, Ian   26–7, 29, 58, 112

Kawai FS610   24, 75
Key, John   50, 55
Korg M1   60–2, 64–5, 67, 84, 117
    patches and presets   65, 71–2, 76
    slap bass patches   71, 76, 85, 97, 99, 100, 103, 105
Korg Wavestation   38, 51, 57, 61, 67

Langley, Ramona   7, 43, 44, 52
    Floral Shoppe (Macintosh Plus)   48, 51, 62, 110
    PrismCorp Virtual Enterprises   3, 52
    情報デスク VIRTUAL   43, 45
Lee, Kerry Ann   23, 28
LinnDrum   60–2, 65–7, 76

Lopatin, Daniel (Oneohtrix Point Never)   6, 48
Lower Hutt   15–16, 18–21, 25, 78, 104
    Queensgate mall   19–20, 22
    as a site of utopias   18–19, 22, 37
A Low Hum   29, 30, 112, 119

Miami Vice   93–5
MIDI (Musical Instrument Digital Interface)   24, 58–61, 71, 76, 120
    MIDI controllers   72–3
    MIDI generators   73–4, 76, 91, 100
millennials; see vaporwave
    as digital natives   10–11, 20, 25, 117
    impact of GFC on   54–5
    shared experiences   10, 20, 98
MOD tracker music   24, 26, 27, 59–60
Mothersbaugh, Mark   101–2
MP3.com   27, 34, 112
music software   1, 11, 12, 36, 57–60; see also digital audio workstations; Jeskola Buzz; MOD tracker music; plug-ins; Virtual Studio Technology
Muzak; see background music

Napster   11, 109
Negativland   9, 23, 36, 101
new age music   3, 31, 40, 65, 68, 92, 99, 105, 107–8, 129
new jack swing   83–4, 96
New Zealand   5, 15, 18–19, 52, 54–5, 70
    1980s economic changes   20–2, 25, 104, 105
New Zealand music   5–6, 49, 114–15, 129
Nirvana   8, 22
Nuendo   58–60, 74, 77, 94, 102, 120

plug-ins   59–60, 73–4, 77; see also Virtual Studio Technology
Post, Mike   68, 105
postirony   8–10; see also under BUY NOW; Eyeliner; vaporwave

record labels   4, 11, 109, 112–13, 118, 119, 124
Reddit   3, 41, 47, 116, 125
    r/makingvaporwave   66–7
    r/vaporwave   4, 47, 49, 116, 127
Rose Quartz   45, 49

Rowell, Luke; see Disasteradio; Eyeliner
    Alexander Turnbull Library archive   12–13, 79, 125–6
    and computers   16–17, 24, 29, 31, 58, 60
    freelance work   33–4, 70–2, 124
    independent approach   27, 28, 112–14
    Internet's influence on   6, 24–7, 34–5
    knee injury   50, 51, 63, 104
    musical influences   15, 17–18, 22–3, 30–2, 34, 131
    music career   5, 6, 11, 112–13, 124
    open-source ethos   27, 52, 124, 125
    university studies   28–9, 36, 40
Rowell, Tom   22–3

samples and sampling; see vaporwave
    recordings of instruments   61, 62, 76–7
    remix culture   125
    technology of   11, 24, 58, 59, 65, 66 n.20
    unauthorized use of   126
    voice samples   2, 28, 80–1, 96, 102–3

Seinfeld 8, 60–1, 64, 71, 76, 117
shopping malls 3, 4, 15, 20–2, 48–9, 69
Skyranch 33–4, 54, 59, 78, 110, 128
slap bass 2, 60–4, 66, 81; *see also* Korg M1
Spotify 121–4
Steely Dan 8, 63–4
synthesizers 2, 7, 11, 17, 57, 108; *see also individual models*
   affordances of 31, 74–5
   efficiencies created by 75–7, 93
   emulations of (*see* Virtual Studio Technology)
   Moog synthesizer albums 15, 16, 23
   and timbral conformity 11, 64–5
   at Victoria University School of Music 28–9
synthpop 23, 30–1, 60, 64, 75, 82

Taylor, Chloe Rose 60–1, 80, 118
television 16, 18, 20, 25
   music 7, 18, 69, 93, 94, 104–5
   music production 39, 75
   shows 8, 27, 101–2 (*see also individual shows*)
Tonelli, Chris 36, 40, 53
Tumblr 3, 34, 47

Unsolved Mysteries 17–18, 94

vaporwave 2–5, 7–8, 41–9, 127–8, 131–2
   archives of 4, 113, 124, 127
   critique of capitalism 3–4, 7–8, 12, 43–4, 53–5, 116
   early examples 34–6, 42, 43, 47–8
   "essentials" 41, 47–8, 116
   Japanese influence 98
   meaning of name 4, 44
   and millennials 6–7, 9, 10, 122, 131–2
   musical sources 3, 7, 42–3, 53, 117
   New Zealand artists 39, 49
   and nostalgia 4, 8, 116, 118
   "nostalgia genre continuum" 35, 42, 47
   online subculture 2, 3, 10, 41, 47–9 (*see also* Reddit)
   and postirony 8–10, 46–8
   production techniques 3, 42–3, 51–2, 62
   sample-free style 3, 52
   subgenres 4, 48–9, 52

use of samples 3, 35, 36, 43, 49, 63, 118
and utopianism 4, 18, 43, 46, 47, 54–5
visual style 3, 127
Victoria University of Wellington (VUW) 28–9, 36
Virtual Studio Technology (VST) 59–60, 91, 131
VSTi plug-ins 60–2, 66–8, 71, 126

Ward, Simon 33–4, 37, 60
Wellington 5, 15, 16, 37, 50, 78
  music scene 22–4, 27–9, 50
Weta 33, 70
Wieden+Kennedy 70, 101
wine 86–7

Yamaha DX7 64–5, 67, 90
YouTube 116–17, 121, 126, 127–8